THE NEW COLOPHON

A Book Collectors' Quarterly

VOLUME 1, PART FOUR
PUBLISHED OCTOBER
1948, NEW YORK

Copyright, 1948, by Duschnes Crawford, Inc.
ALL RIGHTS RESERVED

Printed in the United States of America
by The Anthoensen Press, Portland, Maine

THE NEW COLOPHON

Contents: Volume 1, Part Four, October 1948

JOHN BROWN: HIS HAND AND PEN Boyd B. Stutler	321
RUDYARD KIPLING: TWO FOOTNOTES	
1. "THE PEN TOOK CHARGE." DeLancey Ferguson	335
2. HATCHERS-OUT OF TALES. J. E. Scott	348
THE "PRESENTATION" *Paradise Lost* James Thorpe	357
LITHOGRAPH PROOF BY BENTON SPRUANCE	366
MR. THOREAU WRITES A BOOK James Playsted Wood	367
ROBERT WALDEGRAVE AND THE PIRATES OF DUNKIRK Curt F. Bühler	377
THE PINCHPENNY BIBLIOPHILE Barrows Mussey	383
JEFFERSON, FRENEAU, AND THE *Poems* OF 1809 William Peden	394
THE COURT OF APPEALS	401
MARGINALIA	408
INDEX	423

THE NEW COLOPHON *is published quarterly by* DUSCHNES CRAWFORD INC., *66 East 56th Street, New York 22, N. Y. Fifteen Dollars for the Year.*

The Editors   Elmer Adler   Frederick B. Adams, Jr.

               John T. Winterich

Contributing Randolph G. Adams   Thomas H. Johnson
Editors
                Frank Altschul   Alfred A. Knopf

                Paul M. Angle   Karl Kup

                Paul A. Bennett   Oscar Lewis

                Jacob Blanck   Wilmarth S. Lewis

                Joseph Blumenthal   Flora B. Ludington

                John Carter   A. Hyatt Mayor

                E. De Golyer   Christopher Morley

                Edith Diehl   David A. Randall

                W. A. Dwiggins   Bruce Rogers

                Samuel T. Farquhar   Mrs. Roswell Skeel, Jr.

                Alfred Hamill   Thomas W. Streeter

                Jean Hersholt   Carl I. Wheat

                Philip Hofer   George P. Winship

                Dard Hunter   Lawrence C. Wroth

                Joseph Henry Jackson   Carl Zigrosser

                William A. Jackson

John Brown: His Hand and Pen

By BOYD B. STUTLER

THE life span of John Brown of Osawatomie and Harper's Ferry covered only fifty-nine troubled years from his birth at Torrington, Connecticut, on May 9, 1800, to his untimely taking off from a scaffold at Charles Town, (West) Virginia, on December 2, 1859. His place in the history of his time is a disputed one, depending largely, to the individual, on which side grandpa fought on in the Civil War. But whether he is regarded as firebrand or liberator, there is full agreement among collectors that his letters and documents are hard to come by.

Yet during Brown's lifetime he wrote thousands of letters (how many is anyone's guess), signed his name to hundreds of documents, and filled many notebooks with memoranda. Of all this volume, probably fewer than five hundred pieces survive. This, indeed, is probably a liberal estimate.

Fires, floods, wars, and plain carelessness have all contributed to this scarcity—from the destruction of the homes of Jason and John Brown, Jr., by Border Ruffians in Kansas in 1856, down to the London blitz of 1940. But the chief factor was the great purge of 1859, when most of Brown's associates ran to cover after the Harper's Ferry *putsch,* scoured their files, and destroyed every scrap of writing that would identify them with the man or his mission. The Chicago fire of 1871 helped things along with the destruction of the Horace White and Harvey B. Hurd files, and the following year more Brown material was lost in the great Boston fire.

Moreover, anyone who set out today to build up a John Brown collection would find himself up against stiff competition from institutional and public libraries, which have acquired much material over the years, generally by gift or trade.

In *The Collector* (New York) for December, 1891, Frank D. Andrews suggested the desirability of rounding up letters of the sixty-two signers to the "Declaration of Sentiments" adopted at the organization of the American Anti-Slavery Society at Philadelphia in 1833. In calling the roll of these worthies, Whittier and Garrison among them, he wrote: "But overshadowing them all, and a name that will live in the nation's war songs, is that of John Brown the martyr. Letters of John Brown are rare and the collector is fortunate who secures one. They command the highest price of the anti-slavery agitators."

John Brown's name was thrown into this discussion obviously for good measure, for he was not a member of the Philadelphia group, and in all of his later plots and conspiracies he had little to do with the organized anti-slavery societies. He lone-wolfed it, more or less picked his own crowd, of whom only a few were active Garrisonians. His plans called for direct action; he had little patience with the talking campaigns of the organized anti-slavers. "All talk and no cider" and "great cry but little wool" were two of his barbed comments on the activities of the non-resistant, non-voting Constitution-burners.

When Andrews wrote his *Collector* comment he was probably thinking of the bales upon bales of letters and papers of the Abolitionists through which dealers and librarians were patiently searching for hoped-for nuggets. He knew, too, what a gabby, windy lot these reformers had been, and how they had poured out their troubled souls in a never-ending stream of pleas, prayers, protests, and petitions. All things concerned them, from the abolition of slavery, temperance, and women's rights on through a long maze of crack-pot ideas. Their breed did not die out with the Emancipation Proclamation, the Eighteenth Amendment, or the Noble Experiment that backfired all through the 'twenties. Their souls go marching on. A whole covey of their spiritual chicks can be flushed almost anywhere in America today.

Of the very oldest New England stock (if not a *Mayflower* descendant, then certainly of the second wave), John Brown was brought up in Hudson, Ohio, a small town set in the wilderness of the Western Reserve that was only five years old when Owen Brown took up his residence there. Here was the cultural background of New England, with schools and churches following directly after the first settlers had raised their cabins. The youngster had the benefit of these schools, at least until he had grown to such size that his labor was needed at home. Largely self-taught, however, he acquired the use of words and the facility for stringing them together in strong, pithy phrases. But these flashes could not be long maintained in his letters and propagandizing, where the clear stream of his prose was frequently roiled by the interjection of pious exhortation and scriptural injunction.

One of the best examples of Brown's propaganda writing is his "Farewell to Plymouth Rocks, Bunker Hill Monuments, Charter Oaks and Uncle Toms Cabbins," written in April, 1857, while he was hiding in the home of Judge Thomas Russell of Boston. The "Farewell" was written in the hope that Theodore Parker would read it to his congregation, and thus quicken interest in the Kansas "incident" and produce funds for the war chest. Parker did not read the script from his pulpit. Brown gave a copy to Mrs. George L. Stearns, of Boston, who was so impressed that she set about to convince her husband that he should sell the family home and award the proceeds to John Brown and Kansas. "Mr. Stearns was not quite prepared to sell his estate as she suggested," writes Robert Penn Warren,[1] "and so he compromised by writing a check for $7,000. The two paragraphs of 'Old Brown's Farewell' are one of the highest paid literary productions on record."

John Brown's writing was usually small and clearly formed, though a bit pinched and pointed, and there was little change in the general characteristics of his script from young manhood to as far as he got toward old age. He had his own notions of spelling, and his punctuation was equally individualistic. In his "war" letters to his associates and to members of his family he frequently indulged in double-talk, but there is no known instance in which he ever resorted

[1] Robert Penn Warren in *John Brown: The Making of a Martyr* (New York, 1929), p. 241.

Old Browns Farewell: to the Plymouth Rocks; Bunker Hill, monuments, Charter Oaks; and Uncle Toms Cabbins.

Has left for Kansas. Was trying since he came out of the territory to secure an outfit; or in other words the means of arming and equiping thoroughly; his regular minuet men: who are mixed up with the people of Kansas: and he leaves the States; with a deep feeling of sadness: that after having exhausted his own small means: and with his family and his brave men: suffered hunger, nakedness, cold, sickness, (and some them) imprisonment, with most barbarious, and cruel treatment: wounds, and death: that after lying on the ground for Months; in the most unwholesome and sickly; as well as uncomfortable places: with sick and wounded destitute of any shelter; a part of the time dependant(in part)on the care, and hospitality of Indians: and hunted like Wolves: that after all this; in order to sustain a cause, which every Citizen of this "Glorious Republic," is under equal Moral obligation to do: and for the neglect of which he will be held accountable to God:) in which every Man, Woman, and Child of the entire human family; has a deep and awful interest: that when no wages are asked, or expected: he canot secure (amidst all the wealth, luxury, and extravagance of this "Heaven exalted" people;) even the necessary supplies, for a common Soldier. "How are the mighty fallen"?

John Brown

Boston April, 1857

THIS DOCUMENT BROUGHT $7,000—FOR THE WARS IN KANSAS

to a code, even though "John Brown's cypher" has been hawked about in various forms for a number of years. (It is possible that one of his young intellectuals, Realf or Redpath, the Englishmen, or Cook or Kagi, employed code.) But then, one can buy John Brown's spectacles in two or more places, and examples have actually been sold. The purchasers had probably not read Brown's letter to his cousin Luther Humphrey, written a few days before the execution, in which he offers pious thanks that he had never been driven to the use of glasses.

The Kansas warrior bore a common name. The Veterans Administration has individual files for 6,700 John Brown veterans of American wars. There was no good reason why anyone, in Brown's early life, should have treasured his written words. Brown's letter writing probably began in the winter of 1816-1817 when he spent a few months at Morris Academy in his native Litchfield County, Connecticut, aiming to prepare himself for the ministry. An eye infection soon sent him back to the farm and tannery at Hudson. No letter of this period seems to have been preserved. The first letters found, and, strangely enough, they have been almost entirely ignored by biographers, are those to Seth Thompson, an early business associate, starting in 1826 and continuing until 1849, a run of fifty-five all relating to business and family affairs.[2] It was during this period (1828 to 1835) that John Brown served as postmaster at Randolph, Pennsylvania, his only public office, and not only signed and franked his own letters, but placed his signature as postmaster on all of the letters written by his neighbors. These franks are excessively rare.

Long absences from his home after 1835, ever-widening business interests, bankruptcy, the Kansas war and his conspiratorial activities kept him closely tied to his traveling writing desk. More than a hundred letters were written in the Charles Town jail during the six weeks between the close of his trial and the execution. These letters, naturally, are the prime desiderata of collectors, but only a few of them are in private hands today. Institutional collections have most of them.

The early letters are all signed with Brown's full name, but as he became immersed in plots and conspiracies he resorted to *noms de*

[2] This collection is in the library of Atlanta University, Atlanta, Georgia.

guerre, sometimes an initial which might not be his own, or not signing at all, leaving his correspondent to identify the writer by content or by the distinctive script. Dozens of letters were signed James M. Bell, Nelson Hawkins, James Smith, Isaac Smith, Shubel Morgan, Old Hundred, and at least one by the firm name of Calm & Still. This practice in later years caused the unwitting destruction of many pieces.

For a quarter of a century Brown moved restlessly over the country, buying wool, driving cattle and sheep from New England to as far west as Illinois, surveying in (West) Virginia, making overland wagon trips to Kansas and return, conspiring in Canada, and later ranging over nearly all of the anti-slave states in the interest of his "greatest or principal object." Thus letters were dated from various places in many states. This factor, too, caused the loss of much correspondence because of the inability of many people to identify John Brown of Rockford, Illinois, with cattle to sell, or John Brown of Chatham, Canada West, who writes about cutting cedars on his farm, as the same man who "led a little company of his own" in a midnight raid on the Pottawatomie.

Most important of all his associations were his relations with his own picked crowd, that little group of distinguished anti-slavery men whom he brought together as his "secret committee of six," and who, through the goodness of their souls and implicit faith in Brown's sincerity of purpose, furnished most of the arms and nearly all the capital required to carry on his war in Kansas and prepare for the climax at Harper's Ferry. These were Theodore Parker, most eminent of Boston ministers of his day; Dr. Samuel G. Howe, old Greek revolutionary, philanthropist, and teacher of the blind; George L. Stearns, Boston merchant and manufacturer; Thomas Wentworth Higginson, militant Worcester minister who later commanded a regiment of colored troops in the Southern campaigns; Gerrit Smith, who spread his largess with royal hand from his baronial estate at Peterboro, New York; and Franklin Benjamin Sanborn, an impressionable young chap just out of Harvard who had set up a school at Concord, Massachusetts, and was the intimate of Emerson, Thoreau, Alcott and others of the

Concord group. These men, from early in 1857 until mid-October, 1859, were bombarded with letters by their co-conspirator, and most of these messages were potentially loaded with TNT. Unfortunately, we know of most of this correspondence only by hearsay—most of it vanished in the great purge that followed close upon the news from Harper's Ferry.

There was consternation in Boston and fright in Peterboro when news of the failure of the raid came over the wires. Members of the secret committee figuratively—most of them literally—ran to cover. They had not known John Brown's exact plans, they explained; they only knew that he planned to attack slavery somehow, somewhere, in the South. Gerrit Smith, Sanborn, and Howe began the great cleanup. "I spent hours searching my papers to destroy such as might compromise other persons," Sanborn wrote in his *Recollections*. But he omitted to say that he also destroyed all those that might compromise himself.

"Immediately after the Harper's Ferry affair he (Gerrit Smith) destroyed all the letters touching Brown's movements which he had received from persons in any degree privy to those movements, and he took it for granted that his own similar letters to others had also been destroyed," wrote Mrs. Smith to Sanborn in 1874. Smith did such a good job that in more than four-score years only two or three of Brown's letters to him have come to light, and they are innocuous documents relating to land sales. That he had had a fat file is evidenced by the folder in which they were kept, which is now in Syracuse University Library. It is docketed in Smith's unmistakable hand: "John Brown the Great and Good."

In order to make absolutely certain that nothing had escaped, Smith sent his son-in-law, Colonel Charles Miller, to Boston and Worcester, and as far west as Dorset, Ohio, the home of John Brown, Jr., to root out any scrap of writing that remained. Nothing to incriminate members of the "secret committee of six" was left at the Brown family home at North Elba, New York, for when Wendell Phillips returned to Boston after burying Brown in the shadow of a great rock near his own dooryard, he carried with him a bundle of letters written by Stearns,

Sanborn, Howe, and presumably Smith.[3] Smith was committed to the insane asylum at Utica, New York; Howe, Stearns, and Sanborn went to Canada to wait for the storm to blow over. The militant Thomas Wentworth Higginson stood pat at Worcester. He did not destroy his papers, and he raised his voice with Emerson and Thoreau in defense of John Brown. Theodore Parker, the other member of the committee, was dying of tuberculosis in Italy.

Frederick Douglass, the Negro orator, was at Philadelphia when the Army of Liberation swooped down on Harper's Ferry. He also had been privy to the plot, and a few days before the raid had conferred with Brown in an old stone quarry near Chambersburg, Pennsylvania. He also took cover. From Hoboken, where he laid up for a few days, he sent an unsigned wire to his home in Rochester, New York, asking his son to secrete all his papers. "I was somewhat uneasy from the fact that sundry letters and a Constitution written by John Brown were locked up in my desk," he says in his *Autobiography*. The papers were saved, only to be lost when his Rochester home burned in 1872.

Members of Brown's own family did no purging immediately, but they were soon subjected to the importunities of pestilent autograph collectors, most of whom wanted only a signature to paste in an album. Dozens of family letters were mutilated and their sale value immeasurably impaired by clipping the bottom part of the letter, or chopping the signature out of the sheet. Brown was a thrifty soul who used both sides of the paper; thus, when the signature was clipped, part of the letter on the opposite side was destroyed. As an example of how far this vandalism went, the papers of John Brown, Jr., in the library of the Ohio Archaeological and Historical Society at Columbus may be cited. Of sixty-seven original letters written by the raider now in these files, the signatures of twenty-five have been hacked out.

"How thoughtless all our family were to cut out of father's precious letters his autograph, without in many instances even a postage stamp to pay for sending it. We have been taxed in this way until we positively refused to give away any more of them. You, my dear friend,

---

[3] Atlanta University has the Sanborn letters to Brown; 16 of the Stearns letters are in the Stutler collection; those of Howe and Smith were destroyed. Higginson's papers are in the Boston Public Library.

have been more than generous with us," wrote Ruth Brown Thompson in 1893 to Frank G. Logan, of Chicago, by way of apology for sending him a bobtailed letter. Mr. Logan's fine John Brown collection went to the library of the Chicago Historical Society some thirty years later.

Signature fiends were not the only ones who importuned the Brown family for letters. Many "advanced" collectors wrote the sons and daughters, offering soft soap and blandishments, but rarely cash. There were exceptions. Byron Reed, a coin collector of Omaha, Nebraska, in the middle 'nineties bought five letters at ten dollars each. Four of these are preserved in the Omaha Public Library. Although usually hard-pressed for cash, the family did not make a practice of selling until old age overtook them, and as late as November 10, 1887, John Brown, Jr., had written Ernest C. Brown, of Philadelphia: "So great has been the demand for my father's autograph and the desire of his family to gratify friends in their requests of this sort, that our supply is almost exhausted. We have not, to my knowledge, ever sold one of them, and probably never shall."

Another incident of wangling is told in full in letters in my own cabinet. Back in 1874 W. W. Crannell of Albany, New York, got on the trail. Jason, a son, told him that all the letters he had had were burned in Kansas, and such as he had received later were burned with his home in Ohio in 1860. He referred the inquirer to his sister. The next letter is from Ruth Brown Thompson, who came through with a gift piece. "I send you one of my dear father's letters," she wrote. "It is one I prize on account of the reference he made to Gerrit Smith's election to Congress, and many times have wished that it had been published." The letter came to light again in the Crannell sale in 1931, where it brought $42.50, a full half-dollar over the auction-room average for fifty years.

Frank D. Andrews was probably right when he told in *The Collector* in 1891 of the general scarcity of John Brown autographs, but it is also probably true that the supply was more abundant some twenty years later. The original recipients of letters and documents were still holding on to their treasures, continuing down to the second generation. The business letters to Colonel Simon Perkins were still reposing in the files kept by his children at Akron, Ohio. This big collection was broken up in the middle 'nineties when the improvident Jason— the dreamer who pioneered in heavier-than-air flying machines—was trying to finance another trip to California, and obtained an armload of the papers from the old Colonel's daughter, perhaps forty or fifty of them. These he sold at five dollars each, and as late as February 8, 1897, he wrote Charles E. Chapman from Ben Lomond, California, that he was sending eleven letters and had seventeen left in his hands, offering Chapman a commission of fifty cents for each sale at five dollars.

Jason's little flyer in the autograph business, however (though his activities serve to explain the widespread distribution today of the business letters to Perkins), was not the first direct-sale campaign conducted by a member of the family. This honor went to Salmon, youngest of the surviving sons, who had prospered as a sheep rancher in northern California, but who had been brought to the verge of bankruptcy in the spring of 1891 by the loss of eight thousand of his sheep. This calamity was further aggravated by the decline in market prices of sheep and wool. Salmon turned to the cache of family letters to pull himself out of the hole and in the fall of 1891, with the help of an agent, engineered a deal whereby Ferdinand J. Dreer, noted Philadelphia collector, paid $1,000 for John Brown's last will and codicil, the memorandum for inscription on the old family gravestone, and two letters written from the Charles Town prison. All these, together with a great mass of related "archival estrays" from the Virginia files, are in the Dreer Collection in the Pennsylvania Historical Society. A few years later Major Horatio N. Rust, who had helped Brown to complete the deal for the manufacture of pikes for Harper's Ferry, undertook to relieve the wants of two other members of the family by disposing of treasured letters.

The tremendous volume of letters sent to Brown in prison not only taxed the local postal facilities, but also placed a heavy strain on the staff of censors set up by the civil and military authorities. Many of the letters, perhaps the biggest portion, were requests for autographs.

Many were from anonymous writers who commended or condemned. According to his jailer, Captain John Avis, the anonymous communications were burned unread—unread by Brown. But with a fine eye to the propaganda value of his written words, Brown was highly selective in picking out the letters to be answered among the signed communications. The prison letters were released to the press by the recipients almost as soon as they were received.

Some of Brown's very best letters, including that to Lora Case, of Hudson, Ohio, which was written less than an hour before he left the jail for the scaffold, were in response to requests for something in his own hand. Hiram O'Bannon, one of the jail guards, who had probably rendered the prisoner some small favor, asked for an autograph. Brown promised to comply with the request with the stipulation that the guard should make no commercial use of any writing given him, but did not immediately furnish the desired document. O'Bannon assumed the matter was forgotten, but as the condemned was leaving the jail he handed O'Bannon a strip of paper with a five-line note—now known as "John Brown's Last Prophecy"—which is probably the best known single piece from his pen.[4] It is one Brown item that has been honored by the attention of the professional autograph forger.

Time was running out. While he wrote on day after day, Brown could not get around to all the people he wanted to reach. In letter after letter he asked that copies be made and sent to relatives, friends, or associates. These contemporary copies crop up from time to time to cause confusion, and some have found lodgement in collections in the belief that they are genuine. There is no good reason, however, for historian or collector to be deceived—the copies are not verbatim; no attempt has been made to imitate his handwriting; the letters do not follow Brown's original system of orthography.

Facsimile reproduction is another matter. A lithographed facsimile of a letter to Reverend Luther Humphrey, written from the Charles

[4] It reads: "I, John Brown, am now quite *certain* that the crimes of this *guilty, land: will* never be purged away; but with Blood. I had as *I now think: vainly* flattered myself that without *very much* bloodshed; it might be done." The original is owned by the Chicago Historical Society.

Town jail on November 19, 1859, has been in circulation since about 1880. It is correct in every detail, and is reproduced on paper of the proper period, so that it is little wonder that it has passed readily as an original. Some dozens of copies have found places in library collections through the normal processes. One person is known to have paid $300 for a copy in the assurance that it was the original script. As late as the fall of 1947 another copy of this facsimile was found in an Ohio attic, and was given the usual newspaper publicity. It need only be added that the facsimile was made in complete good faith.[5]

Despite the rarity of his letters, John Brown's auction room performance has not been impressive. One reason is that the best items have never found their way into the auction room. The old covenanter has fared much better in person-to-person and dealer-to-collector negotiations, with at least one piece running up to a respectable four-figure price tag. This was the prison letter to Lora Case, which a New York dealer originally priced at $2,500, but it is understood among the cognoscenti that the late W. T. H. Howe got a liberal discount when he acquired it. The letter passed with his library to the Berg Collection in the New York Public Library.

An analysis of the record as set down in *American Book Prices Current* from 1894 to 1947 reveals that 113 John Brown autographic items have been put on the block; of this number, 17 were repeats, which reduces the total to 96 units. This is an average of slightly more than two sales per year, repeats included. The 113 lots fetched a total of $4,740.75, or an average of $41.95 per item. The pieces ranged in importance from the detached cover of a pocket notebook, signed ($10.50), and a two-line, undated order for a package, both valuable only for the signature, to the original draft of the Provisional Constitution adopted at the convention at Chatham, Canada, in 1858, with a few prison letters. The Provisional Constitution, taken from the files at Richmond after its evacuation by the Confederate government, brought only $52.50 at the Colonel John Trumbull sale in 1897. It would do rather better today.

[5] For a full discussion of the facsimile of the letter to Luther Humphrey, see "John Brown's Letter," by Boyd B. Stutler, in *Colby Library Quarterly*, May, 1947.

The lowest price recorded is that for a letter to Mrs. Brown, undated and with signature clipped, which brought $4.25 at Bangs's in 1896. Two years later, when Stan Henkels put the same letter on the block, someone was ready to raise the ante twenty-five cents. The highest auction price recorded is that for a prison letter to Miss Sterns, of Springfield, Massachusetts, the daughter of an old friend, which brought $352 at Anderson's in 1916. The same letter came up again in the William Harris Arnold sale in 1924, when it brought only $135. All traces of some of the 96 auctioned units have been lost; some are still in private collections, but the greater portion have gone into public or institutional libraries, usually by gift.

The papers of John Brown, Jr., now in the Ohio State Archaeological and Historical Society, comprise hundreds of separate items, filling nine file-boxes, all bearing on the activities of John Brown and his family. This library stands at the top of the list in its holdings of original John Brown letters and documents with 67 pieces, not including the Springfield (Massachusetts) wool business letter-book, containing copies of some 1,300 letters. Atlanta University is second with its long run of 55 personal letters to Seth Thompson, and my own collection is third with 40 letters and memoranda. Kansas Historical Society, which became the repository for the family's Kansas papers in 1881, owns 35 original letters and documents, most of which relate to Brown's Kansas interlude. Other important collections are lodged in the Henry E. Huntington Library, San Marino, California, 20 items, including two memorandum books; Chicago Historical Society, 19; Boston Public Library, 13, and two memorandum books; Massachusetts Historical Society, 5, and in the Dreer Collection in Pennsylvania Historical Society and the Villard Collection in Columbia University Library. All of these afford fertile fields for the student and research worker, for in each library the few original John Brown letters and documents are supplemental to an important mass of related material.

The Virginia State Library has five big file boxes crammed with related papers, most of them referring to the trial at Charles Town, but there is not a scrap of John Brown's writing in the lot—it was picked clean by Union soldiers, with an assist from local talent, after the fall of Richmond in April, 1865. Some of the papers "liberated" by these raiders have served to enrich the files of libraries in Northern cities, but most of them, sent home as souvenirs, have been irretrievably lost.

Through the whole Civil War a Richmond Unionist sympathizer, Elizabeth L. Van Lew, served the Federal cause faithfully and well as an agent who organized a competent espionage service. When General Grant moved into the city he immediately detailed a colonel to guard her from the wrath of her fellow-citizens. The guard, after a protracted search, found her in the deserted capitol "seeking in the archives for documents which might otherwise have been destroyed."[6] Some result of her search, signed and dated, crops up now and then, as witness Norman Dodge's *Month at Goodspeed's* for June, 1934, which carries a full-page illustration of the title page of a printed copy of John Brown's *Provisional Constitution and Ordinance* with the written inscription: "Found Among his papers in the capitol April, 1865, by E. L. Van Lew."

What would John Brown have thought of all this pother about his literary remains? We have an inkling, at least, in a portion of a dispatch from Edward H. House, special correspondent, in the *New York Tribune* for November 30, 1859: "Last evening I obtained a permit and with a few others entered the jail and conversed with the occupants of the various cells. . . . He (John Brown) was several times importuned for his autograph, but without avail. He seems to have great repugnance to parting with any of his handwriting. . . . The reason that he gave was that his autograph had been sought, personally and by letter, by hundreds of persons, and that if he should attempt compliance it would deprive him of all the time that remained to him on earth, which he ought to occupy differently."

[6] W. G. Beymer in *On Hazardous Service* (New York, 1912), p. 96.

Rudyard Kipling: Two Footnotes

1. "The Pen Took Charge"

By DeLANCEY FERGUSON

IN recalling his desolate childhood at Southsea, Rudyard Kipling mentioned some early reading which he was never able to identify in after years. "Somehow or other," he said in his autobiography, *Something of Myself* (1937), "I came across a tale about a lion-hunter in South Africa who fell among lions who were all Freemasons, and with them entered into a confederacy against some wicked baboons. I think that, too, lay dormant until the *Jungle Books* began to be born." And then he became specific in describing "two books of verse about child-life" which he could not trace:

One—blue and fat—described "nine white wolves" coming "over the wold" and stirred me to the deeps; and also certain savages who "thought the name of England was something that could not burn."

The other book—brown and fat—was full of lovely tales in strange metres. A girl was turned into a water-rat "as a matter of course"; an Urchin cured an old man of gout by means of a cool cabbage-leaf, and somehow "forty wicked Goblins" were mixed up in the plot; and a "Darling" got out on the house-leads with a broom and tried to sweep stars off the skies. It must have been an unusual book for that age, but I have never been able to recover it.

A few months after the autobiography was published, a correspondent named Victor Bonney announced in the *Kipling Journal*[1] the identification of both volumes, which had been lent him by a Miss Gina Peach of Yorkshire:

... These two books looking exactly as Kipling described them are in front of me as I write. The blue one is entitled *Poems Written for a Child by Two Friends*,

[1] No. 43 (Sept., 1937), pp. 96-97.

and the brown one *Child-Nature by One of the Authors of Child-World*—the actual names of the authors are not given. Both books were published by Strahan and Co., of 56, Ludgate Hill, the blue one in 1868 and the brown one in 1869.

The "nine white wolves" occur in a poem called "A North Pole Story":

> *And as one strode so bold*
> *He saw a sight of fear*
> *Nine white wolves came over the wold*
> *And they were watching a deer.*

The savages occur in a poem called "Heroes," but Kipling's memory slipped here—

> *You should have seen the black men*
> *How grey their faces turn*
> *They think the name of England*
> *Is something that* will *burn.*
>
> [The emphasis is Bonney's.]

In the brown book are all the incidents related in the autobiography; the girl turned into a water-rat, the urchin curing gout by a cabbage-leaf and the Darling who tries to sweep the stars off the sky. To have been able to remember all these things after more than sixty years shows what an extraordinarily retentive memory Kipling must have had. The metre employed in the poems is various, but they all go with a good swing and are still interesting to read....

So far as one may judge from published allusions, whether among the earnest brethren of the Kipling Society or elsewhere, Mr. Bonney's discovery reverberated like Don Marquis's rose-petal in the Grand Canyon. If anyone else has looked at the volumes, he has done so in strict privacy. True, they seem to be excessively rare. Even specialists in children's literature are unacquainted with them; in this country, the only recorded copy of the blue volume is in the New York Public Library, and the brown one is in the Olin Memorial Library at Wesleyan University. Probably most of the copies were read to pieces; that there were at least two editions of *Poems Written for a Child* is proved by the fact that Mr. Bonney's copy was dated 1868 and the New York copy is 1869.

If Mr. Bonney had applied at any good public library, he could easily have identified the authors; if he had been more percipient in looking at the books themselves, he would have discovered some interesting details which Kipling did not mention. At least one of the poems mentioned has more significance than Kipling, or Mr. Bonney, realized, and each volume contains an additional poem which Kipling did not refer to, but which obviously affected him profoundly.

Halkett and Laing, the indefatigable compilers of the *Dictionary of Anonymous and Pseudonymous English Literature,* would have informed Mr. Bonney that the "Two Friends" were Menella Bute Smedley and Mrs. E. A. Hart; the British Museum Catalogue would have told him further that Menella Smedley was born in 1820 and died in 1877. For that matter, Kipling himself could have traced his lost volumes by following a lead from his own library. When he wrote *Something of Myself* he still owned "a bound copy of *Aunt Judy's Magazine* of the early 'seventies, in which appeared Mrs. Ewing's *Six to Sixteen*." That was the volume for Christmas, 1872. Had he ever looked up Volume I (Christmas, 1866), he would have found "A North Pole Story" and other poems signed with Menella Smedley's initials, and with her full name given in the index.

Besides the two volumes we are concerned with, Menella Smedley wrote a whole shelf of prose tales, from *The Maiden Aunt* (1847) to *Other Folks' Lives* (1869), and a volume of *Poems* (1869) for adult readers. This last is shot full of Tennysonian echoes, but includes one poem, "Odin's Sacrifice," which anticipated by a year the Laureate's use of the same legend in "The Victim."

The two "fat" volumes for children measure about 3⅜ by 5⅛ inches. *Poems Written for a Child* has 312 pages and eighteen pictures; *Child-Nature,* 294 pages and sixteen pictures. A considerable part of the earlier volume consists of such lyrics as any Victorian rimester could produce by the bale. But three narrative poems are notable—"A North Pole Story," "Heroes," and "The Wives of Brixham." Quotation will reveal their importance. "A North Pole Story," subtitled "A Fact," opens thus:

Up where the world grows cold,
  Under the sharp North star,
The wrinkled ice is very old
  And the life of man is far;
None to see when the fog falls white,
  And none to shiver and hear
How wild the bears are in the night
  Which lasts for half a year!
. . . .

Earth speaks with awful lips,
  "No place for man is here!
Between my bergs I'll crush your ships,
  If you will come too near;
You shall be slain by bitter wind
  Or starved on barren shore;
My cruel snow shall strike you blind;
  Go,—trouble me no more!"

But British men are fain
  To venture on and through,
And when you tell them to refrain,
  They set themselves to do;
Into the secrets of the snow
  They hurry and they press,
And answer Nature's coldest "No"
  With a great shout of "Yes."

It was a little band
  Went on that dangerous track,
To do a message from our land,
  And to bring an answer back.
The frost had bound their good ship tight,
  And years were come and gone,
When a few brave hearts, as best they might,
  Went over the shores alone.

And as one strode so bold,
  He saw a sight of fear,—
Nine white wolves came over the wold,
  And they were watching a deer;
By three and by two and by one,
  A cunning half-moon they made,
They glanced at each other and did not run,
  But crept like creatures afraid.

The poem then goes on to relate how the wolves drove the deer over a cliff and killed it. Later, the man who had witnessed the hunt was himself surrounded by wolves, but, remembering what he had seen, escaped by boldly walking through the ring instead of retreating before it.

"Heroes" begins by telling how the children had lamented that there were no more heroes—"There never will come knights-errant / To common days like these." Of course, they were reminded, there was Garibaldi, but—Garibaldi was not English. Then the narrator continues:

> Shake not your heads at England,
>   Her soil is still of worth;
> It cannot lose the habit
>   Of bringing heroes forth.
> I met one yesterday evening,
>   And when you hear his tale,
> You'll not be sighing and saying
>   That times are feeble and pale.

Three or four English missionaries in Africa, she says, met a coffle of eighty slaves, and routed the slavers with bold words.

> The night was grave and splendid,
>   A dead queen lying in state,
> With all her jewels upon her,
>   And trumpets at her gate....
>
> Studious men and gentle,
>   But not in the least afraid;
> With fire enough among them
>   To furnish a crusade....
>
> They did not care for treaties,
>   And death they did not fear;
> One great wrong would have roused them,—
>   There were eighty here;
> They were not doing man's work,
>   They were doing the Lord's,
> So they went and stopp'd the savages
>   With these amazing words:—

> "We are three or four English,
>   And we cannot let this be,—
> Get away to your mountains,
>   And set the people free!"
> You should have seen the black men,
>   How grey their faces turn;
> They think the name of England
>   Is something that will burn.

And so the cowed slavers release their captives, and the poem ends with a moral:

> *A glorious gift is Prudence,*
>   *And they are useful friends*
> *Who never make beginnings*
>   *Till they can see the ends;*
> *But give us now and then a man,*
>   *That we may make him king,*
> *Just to scorn the consequence,*
>   *And just to do the thing.*

Here, in a Victorian nursery book, burned into the memory of a lonely child, is the germ of the whole doctrine of the White Man's Burden and the divine mission of the English which so irked the critics of the mature Kipling. And not the ideas merely; the very rhythms of the poem recur in more than one of Kipling's didactic verses, such as "The Wage-Slaves."

But there was another poem which Kipling remembered clearly in 1896, and which it is hard to believe that he had forgotten in 1935. Readers of *Captains Courageous* will remember Disko Troop's aversion to "Skipper Ireson's Ride," and how he sent Harvey Cheyne to forestall the possibility that the "Philadelphia actress-woman might recite the poem at the Memorial Day services. Instead, she read

some sort of poem about a fishing-port called Brixham and a fleet of trawlers beating in against storm by night, while the women made a guiding fire at the head of the quay with everything they could lay hands on.

> "They took the grandam's blanket,
>   Who shivered and bade them go;
> They took the baby's cradle,
>   Who could not say them no."

Rudyard Kipling: Two Footnotes

"Whew!" said Dan, peering over Long Jack's shoulder. "That's great! Must ha' bin expensive, though."

"Ground-hog case," said the Galway man. "Badly lighted port, Danny."

. . . .

> *"And knew not all the while*
> *If they were lighting a bonfire*
> *Or only a funeral pile."*

The wonderful voice took hold of people by their heartstrings; and when she told how the drenched crews were flung ashore, living and dead, and they carried the bodies to the glare of the fires, asking: "Child, is this your father?" or "Wife, is this your man?" you could hear hard breathing all over the benches.

> *"And when the boats of Brixham*
> *Go out to face the gales,*
> *Think of the love that travels*
> *Like light upon their sails!"*

There was very little applause when she finished. The women were looking for their handkerchiefs, and many of the men stared at the ceiling with shiny eyes. . . .

"The Wives of Brixham" fills seven pages of *Poems Written for a Child*, and the stanzas which Kipling quoted from his remarkable but not wholly accurate memory are these:

> *They took the grandame's blanket*
>   *Who shivered and bade them go;*
> *They took the baby's pillow,*
>   *Who could not say them no.*
> *And they heap'd a great fire on the pier,*
>   *And knew not all the while*
> *If they were heaping a bonfire,*
>   *Or only a funeral pile.*
>
> *And, fed with precious food, the flame*
>   *Shone bravely on the black,*
> *Till a cry rang through the people*
>   *"A boat is coming back!"*
> *Staggering dimly through the fog*
>   *Come shapes of fear and doubt;*
> *But when the first prow strikes the pier,*
>   *Cannot you hear them shout?*

Then all along the breadth of flame
  Dark figures shriek'd and ran,
With, "Child, here comes your father!"
  Or, "Wife, is this your man?"
And faint feet touch the welcome stone,
  And wait a little while;
And kisses drop from frozen lips
  Too tired to speak or smile.

So, one by one, they struggled in,
  All that the sea could spare;
We will not reckon through our tears
  The names that were not there;
But some went home without a bed,
  When all the tale was told,
Who were too cold with sorrow
  To know the night was cold.

And this is what the men must do
  Who work in wind and foam;
And this is what the women bear
  Who watch for them at home.
So when you see a Brixham boat
  Go out to face the gales,
Think of the love that travels
  Like light upon her sails!

The "brown and fat" *Child-Nature* is a sort of Canterbury Tales told round the nursery fire by various members of a large family, the tales interspersed with songs and passages of discussion. "Sweeping the Skies" is "Amy's Story," and tells how "Darling" asked what the stars are. Told that

> *If she can give them a tap,*
> *Plates of sky-china emboss'd with star-gold*
> *Softly will slide to her lap,*

she gets a broom and tries to sweep them down. When she can't reach them from a garden chair, she goes up on the roof, but is rescued before she falls off.

"Uncle Ned's Story" of "The Water-Rat" tells of a child who fell into a pond, was changed into a rat, and came home in that form, regaining her natural shape the next day. It ends:

> *Of course a fairy pond was that,*
>   *And she was saved by fairy force,*
> *And changed into a water-rat;*
>   *All these are matters quite of course.*
> *Of course her happy mother wept—*
>   *Her father felt as if he dream'd—*
> *Her brothers ran about and leapt—*
>   *And as for me, of course I scream'd.*

In "Tom's Story" of "Miss Pip," an "'umble Urchin" is sent to carry a love-letter from his master, the Old Commandant, to Miss Pip, the Baron's daughter. The Baron suffers from gout, and announces that he will give his daughter to the man who can cure him. The Commandant proposes strong green tea as a remedy. Mr. Simpkins, a rival suitor, protests that green tea is poison, but is neatly disposed of by the Urchin:

> *Then the 'umble Urchin*
>   *'Umbly answer'd, "Oh,*
> *Civil Mr. Simpkins*
>   *Never could speak so!*
> *Forty wicked demons*
>   *Made a wicked plan—*
> *Put in an appearance—*
>   *Not a real man!*
>
> *"Dearest Mr. Simpkins!*
>   *Absent injured friend!*
> *We are not deluded—*
>   *We foresee the end!*
> *This is not our Simpkins,*
>   *Credit it who can!*
> *This is an appearance,*
>   *Not a real man!"*

Whereupon everyone shrinks away, and poor Simpkins creeps off to die, convinced that he *is* only an appearance, not a man. Then the

CHILD-NATURE

BY ONE OF THE AUTHORS OF
"CHILD-WORLD"

STRAHAN & CO., PUBLISHERS
56 LUDGATE HILL, LONDON
1869

Mowgli's Birthplace

Commandant tries the strong green tea, and it makes the Baron scream.

> *To the castle garden,*
> *At an 'umble trot,*
> *Went the 'umble Urchin—*
> *'Umbly gather'd—what?*
> *'Neath his 'umble jerkin*
> *'Umbly brought it in:*
> *"Now my 'umble cure, sir,*
> *May I just begin?"*
>
> *'Umbly, on the toe, he*
> *Clapp'd a cabbage-leaf:*
> *Baron Pip is laughing*
> *With the quick relief.*
> *Nature's 'umblest herbage*
> *To relieve us springs,*
> *And her 'umble Urchins*
> *Do surprising things!*

So of course it was the Urchin who married Miss Pip. Here, as with "the name of England" passage, Kipling's young mind had not really grasped the full meaning of the phrases he read. Though he knew that forty demons, or goblins, were somehow mixed up in the story, he never understood the true import of the Urchin's strategy.

So much for the poems which Kipling admitted to remembering. *Child-Nature*, however, like the earlier volume, contains a poem which he did not mention, but which in later years helped to produce surprising results. This is "Lucy's Story" of "Wolfie":

> *A wolf took a child in her mouth,*
> *And carried him off to her cave;*
> *And so he grew up among little young wolves,*
> *Who taught him how to behave.*
> *It was a sight most strange and sad*
> *To see the wolves instruct the lad.*
> *And if the lad his turn would try*
> *To teach them gentler manners, why*
> *They'd snarl at him, and at him fly.*

And so as time went on and on,
Impressions left his tender brain;
  He thought he was a wolf anon,
  Nor felt the shame and pain.

  He learn'd to crouch,
    (He liked crouching);
And to slouch,
  (He was fond of slouching);
And to howl,
  (He delighted in howling);
And to prowl,
  (He adored prowling).

He learnt to shamble vilely on all fours,
And live in dim damp places out of doors;
While, of all pleasures that his soul could win,
He liked to show his teeth, and snarl, and grin.

  I found him, and put him to school;
    Was it the act of a fool?
  He couldn't write straight with a rule,
  He ran about clotheless and cool,
And never would sit on a chair or a stool....

But having got thus far with the story, Menella Smedley's inspiration petered out in silliness. The remainder of the poem tells how the wolf-boy took to biting the other boys, and finally ate up the master and was expelled. Reformers and lawyers tried vainly to make him mend his ways. At last

They sent for a woman. Aha!
Poor Wolfie! How altered you are:
You are mild as a lamb that says "Baa!"
You lie at her feet, Wolfie. Ah!
Has nobody guessed—she's the boy's own Mamma!

So the germ of Mowgli, as well as of the White Man's Burden, lies hidden in Menella Smedley's nursery tales, and Kipling's own brief words about the birth of the *Jungle Books* take on additional meaning:

It chanced that I had written a tale about Indian Forestry work which included a boy who had been brought up by wolves. In the stillness, and suspense, of the winter of '92 some memory of the Masonic lions of my childhood's magazine, and a phrase in Haggard's *Nada the Lily,* combined with the echo of this tale. After blocking out the main idea in my head, the pen took charge, and I watched it begin to write stories about Mowgli and animals.

That tale of the Masonic lions still eludes us, as it eluded Kipling. A decade after the *Jungle Books* were written, he appealed, in a letter now in the Berg Collection in the New York Public Library, to Routledge, London publisher of many juveniles, for aid in tracing it, but without success. So far, indeed, even bibliographers have shrunk from the task of cataloguing the mass of juveniles which were produced in the latter half of the nineteenth century. But Rider Haggard's singularly grim and powerful tale of the great Zulu empire of Chaka and Dingaan is easily accessible. Though identification of the precise phrase which Kipling alludes to is impossible, it was somewhere in the two chapters which tell how Galazi and Umslopogaas, fugitives from the wrath of Chaka, became leaders of the pack of Ghost Wolves.

In one episode, for instance, villagers turn upon Galazi:

"He is a wolf—he is a wizard!" they screamed. "Kill him! Kill the wolf-wizard before he brings the ghosts upon us!" And they ran toward me with uplifted spears.

"I am a wolf indeed," I cried, "and I am a wizard indeed, and I will bring wolves and ghosts upon you before all is done." And I turned and fled. . . .

Or again,

"The pack is gathered; now for the hunt!" cried Galazi. . . . And on many a moonlight night they and the wolves hunted together, winning their food. At times they crossed the river, hunting in the plains, . . . and the people of the kraal would come out, hearing the mighty howling, and watch the pack sweep across the veldt, and with them a man or men. Then they would say that the ghosts were abroad and creep into their huts shivering with fear. . . .

Past question, here were suggestions for "Tiger! Tiger!" and "Letting in the Jungle." Any reader who remembers the original illustrations of *The Jungle Book* must recall the picture of Mowgli, silhouetted against the moonrise and followed by the wolves, bearing Shere

Khan's skin on his head on his way to the Council Rock. And one other phrase of Haggard's must not be overlooked. At the close of the Ghost Wolves episode, Galazi and Umslopogaas face ordeal by battle for the chieftancy of the People of the Axe. One of the village elders, watching them before the fight, says:

"These are no cravens that hold the axe and club. They are but lads indeed, yet they have drunk wolf's milk."

The Jungle Books have many other "sources," including *Beast and Man in India* by the author's father, and Phil Robinson's *In an Indian Garden*. But sources do not explain the alchemy of genius which converts them into masterpieces. The important fact is that the first spark which lit the fire had smoldered in Kipling's mind for more than two decades, and it was set there by Menella Bute Smedley.

2. Hatchers-out of Tales

By J. E. SCOTT

Readers of Kipling's *Something of Myself* will remember the reference made there to his friendship with Rider Haggard. "His comings were always a joy to us and the children.... We found by accident that each could work at ease in the other's company. So he would visit me and I him, with work in hand; and between us we could even hatch out tales together—a most exacting test of sympathy." Over twenty years before, Haggard, in *The Days of My Life*, had used the very same term, which expresses so aptly the regard in which they held each other.

The friendship which existed between them was much stronger than is generally known, and more intimate than can be gathered from the slight allusions made to it in their respective autobiographies. Both men had much in common: they were imperialists with an intense love of their country and its well-being; their manner was reserved and somewhat offhand to those whom they did not know well; and they possessed a certain farsightedness and clearness of vision not always given to men, though this was more evident in Haggard than in Kipling. An additional bond cemented them—that of domestic tragedy in the early period of their married lives. Kipling's elder daughter died in New York in 1899, and Haggard's son, on whom he had set so much hope, died suddenly while his father was in Mexico in 1891.

Their first meeting had occurred soon after Kipling arrived in England, but although they corresponded from time to time and met at many literary functions, their friendship did not really develop until 1902, after Kipling had settled at Bateman's, Burwash.

Until that time, their literary pursuits had kept them apart; Kipling went to South Africa, Japan, Canada, and America, Haggard to Egypt, Cyprus, and Iceland. Throughout his life Rider Haggard always carried in his pocket a little notebook in which he used to jot down such details as appointments, addresses, and ideas and plots for stories. Some thirty-five of these notebooks—the first dated 1874, when he was eighteen, the last 1925 (he died on May fourteenth of that year) —are still in existence. Although the notebooks are in no sense diaries of day-to-day experiences, Haggard frequently wrote down, in addition to the details mentioned, his impressions of countries, characters, and places, the notables he had met, and fragments of his conversation with them. He records, for example, in the notebook for 1905 his first meeting with Theodore Roosevelt and a good deal of their talk.

In the notebook for 1904 there are two versions of a contemplated story which later appeared in March, 1906, under the title of *The Way of the Spirit,* and this seems to be the first of many of Haggard's stories in which Kipling took an interest and discussed plot and theme with the author. Writing to Haggard on December 2, 1904, having read and returned the manuscript, Kipling said:

> The only criticism I venture to make is that it should end on the words "Her lord's bed." I don't think Lady Devene's text at the end strengthens an already immensely strong situation. For the rest I did what I have done with a many of your

books—simply surrendered myself to the joy of reading and read on. That's better than any criticism.

And to Haggard's answer, he replied on the fifth:

I knew you'd take my criticism (such as it was) in good part. It's only a question of what note you end on—her love for her lord or the moral of the whole tale and *that* (i.e. that there is a God who punishes etc.) is so strongly pointed out throughout that it seemed to me better, perhaps, to end on the simple human sexual love.

But the book, which was dedicated to him, appears to have impressed Kipling considerably, for he referred to it again two months after its publication. On May 28, 1906, he wrote:

I've been reading over *The Way of the Spirit* again—it's a book that stands re-reading—and it has just occurred to me that the woman of the West wouldn't have been so impressed by the woman of the East to the extent of admitting her *moral* superiority. Do you think I'm right?

I mean admitting it at once as she practically does. Question is, wouldn't she have made a bigger fight against the idea than she did? I'm a little curious on the subject.

A footnote to the above letter contains the following query: "Have you done anything to your tree yarn?" This refers to *The Ghost Kings*, originally called *The Shapes*, of which further evidence of Kipling's interest in Haggard's works exists in the form of short manuscript notes of the plot of the story in the handwriting of the two men. This plot consists of three quarto pages, with Kipling and Haggard writing alternate paragraphs.

Kipling begins with a contribution which takes the story up to the point where the Zulus, in desperation at having in their midst a demented girl whose very madness brings disaster upon them in one form or another, decide to take her to the Dingaan, who is anxious to see this person who can subdue his warriors. He orders her to appear before him and his people.

The tale is continued in Haggard's hand. He describes the arrival of the Ghost Kings' messengers, the taking away of Rachel to the north, the great forest, the storm, and her experiences while living

Death's name

Taung) Takht   ) Adm adam
Moung) ~~Tarld~~   ) m a da
Paung) ~~Da~~ Rukhm) Ja
         Mar
         TarKoth   Kōth   Kaf.
         Koth Kôth   ~~Mo~~ Kaf
                      •Salm:
                Murth
         morgue: Murg. Morg:
               Murg   Murg: Murgh: (nonechosen)

BURWASH ETCHINGHAM

BATEMAN'S BURWASH SUSSEX

"On a double sheet of his notepaper, Kipling wrote down several possibilities"

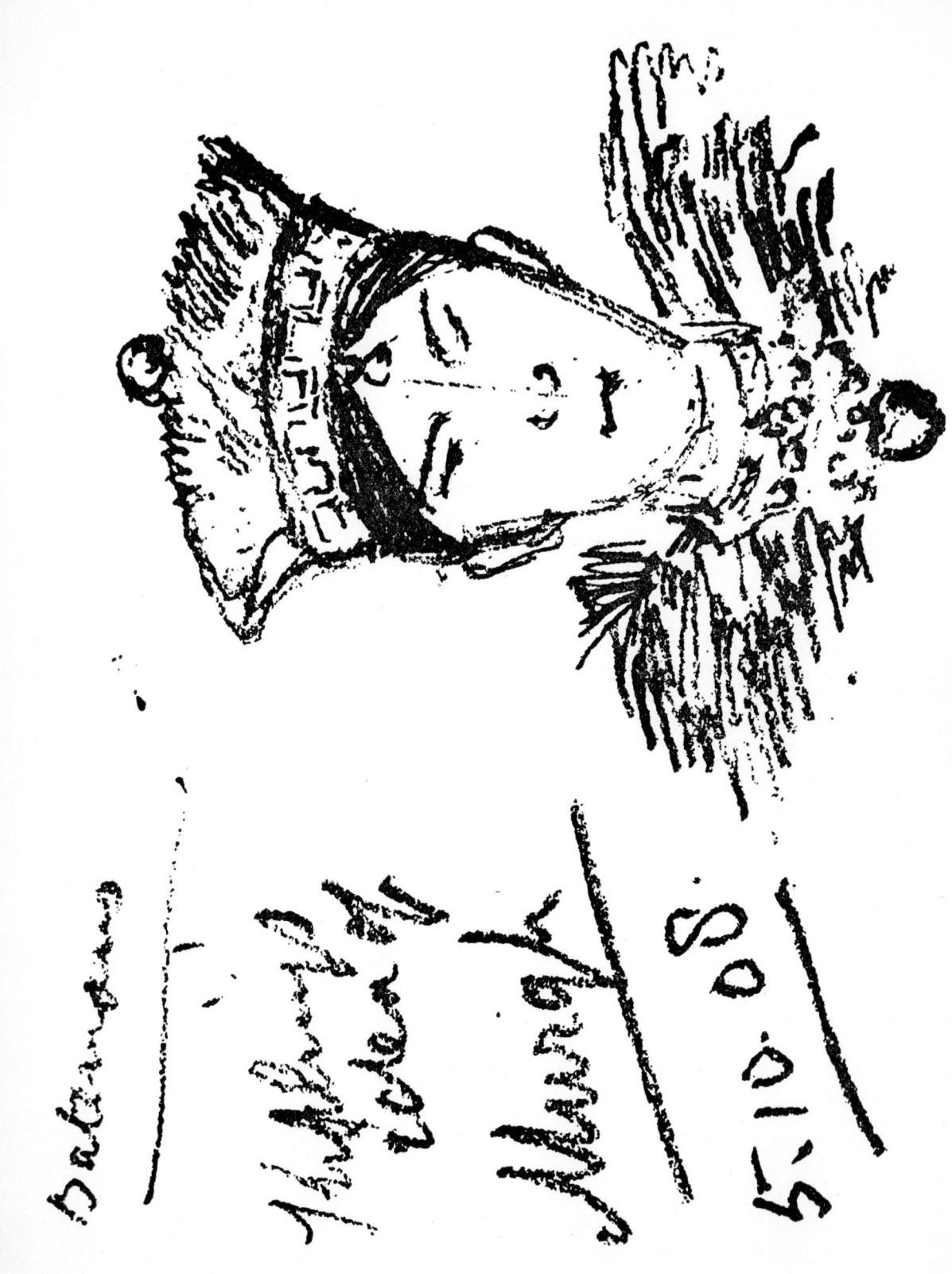

"Kipling drew a pencil sketch of Murgh"

with the ghost people, until finally she meets her lover tied to a tree in the heart of the forest.

The conclusion is provided by Kipling—the battle of wits between Rachel and one of the Ghost Kings (Nyan in the manuscript) for her lover's life and her final victory over Nyan by threatening him with the Red Death (death by the spear), of which he and all his tribe are mortally afraid. This plot, with certain variations, is an expanded version of the first rough draft set down by Haggard in his notebook in February, 1906.

Kipling and Haggard also talked over *Red Eve* together—a historical novel of the time of Edward III dealing with the coming of the Black Death to Europe and thence to England. Throughout the pages of the book stalks the sombre figure of Murgh, the Messenger, the Gateway of the Gods, who wore a strange headdress:

a cap fitting tight to the skull, only running across the crown of it was a stiff raised ridge, of leather perhaps, jagged and pointed, something like the comb of a cock. This comb . . . was surmounted at its highest point by a ball of black of the size of a small apple. The cap itself was yellow, except its lowest band. . . . In the centre of this band upon the forehead glowed a stone like a ruby.

This description is in all probability Kipling's, for he drew a small pencil sketch of the head of Murgh to show the type of thing he meant, at the side of which Haggard wrote "Kipling's idea of Murgh, 5.10.08." Between them, too, they evolved a suitable name for this character of Death; on a double sheet of his own printed notepaper, Kipling wrote down several possibilities until the word *morgue,* with its contractions to *morg, mung, murg,* gave them the name they wanted and finally used: Murgh.

It is clear from many of Kipling's letters to Haggard that he had the opportunity of reading the manuscripts of several other stories: *Child of Storm, The Wanderer's Necklace* ("Herewith the MS. The Necklace I like *immensely.* It's all you with a rush and a whirl and holds like all the others of yours"), *When the World Shook* ("Here's your MS. back again and a thousand thanks for the privilege. . . . My only criticism is that I don't quite like the essential clumsiness and angularity of Bastin. It's indicated all right but I want it brought out more in the various situations").

Others, such as *The Ivory Child, Finished, The Virgin of the Sun,* he read as soon as they were published, and he was continually writing to Haggard commenting on his "amazing freshness" and "flowing vitality" which "always hits me between my envious eyes."

The plot of another surviving story is similar in construction to that of *The Ghost Kings*. It is the "Tale of Beginnings," *Allan and the Ice-Gods,* the last adventure of Allan Quatermain to be published. These manuscript notes consist of four quarto pages; the first (which has been added at a later date but is listed here because it completes the whole tale) is written by Haggard. He relates how Lady Ragnall bequeathed the "taduki" herb to Allan, Allan's doubts about the wisdom of accepting it, his temptation and fall, up to the point in his vision when he recognizes himself as Wi, the chieftain of a tribe of some fifty souls living in the remote Ice Age.

On the second page is a rough sketch by Kipling of the glacier which plays so prominent a part, with a small bay at the foot and seals lying about on ice floes. Down the left-hand side of this drawing, and extending in some cases halfway across it, is a list of the names of the characters in the story, with an explanation of their meaning: i.e. Moananga, avaricious; Whaka, a bird of ill omen, one who howls, etc. The entire page is written in pencil by Kipling.

He has changed this for a pen, however, on the third page, and sets out the history of the tribe, its beliefs and superstitions, a description of the valley where it is situated, and a small plan to illustrate the gradual forward movement of the glacier itself. This page is ended by Haggard's description of how Wi determines to save his people by some means.

The fourth and last page is written by both authors. Kipling describes Wi's journey to the top of the mountain, his long vigil there and his communing with the god (a mammoth embalmed in the ice) and with his own soul; the sudden conception of a plan to save the tribe, and the realization of all the trouble and danger he will have to bear in his attempts to carry this out. Haggard concludes with the setting out of Wi's party into the unknown, the designs of the witch Laleela, and Wi's final self-sacrifice.

On the back of this last page is a note in Haggard's hand: "Synopsis of Story drawn up by Rudyard K. and myself at Bateman's. Febry. 1922. H. RIDER HAGGARD."

This paper in no way intends to suggest that Kipling contributed more than Haggard to these plots, for it would be entirely wrong to judge each man's share merely by the amount each happens to have written. What took place during such discussions was likely to have been the normal procedure of any friends under such circumstances; one wrote down on paper each stage of the plot so far as it had been evolved between them, and, after a time, handed it over to the other, who carried the tale further with his friend's help.

Yet this interest on Kipling's part in Haggard's works was by no means one-sided, for the latter in his turn used to discuss Kipling's plots and the work he happened to have in hand. Writing in his notebook for 1911 under date of September 30 (he had gone to Bateman's for the week end), Haggard says:

> We talked a great deal on many subjects, making plots for books etc. He read me some of his plays and we discussed others, especially one that would deal with the fall of the British Empire.
>
> I went through the plot of *The Mahatma and the Hare* with him. He thought it a fine thing and said I should have carried it further and answered the argument of the hare with the instance of the sufferings of mankind at the hands of a power as superior to it as we are to the hare. I replied that such things have a limit....
>
> On Sunday and Monday I sat in his study while he worked and after a while he got up and remarked to me that my presence did not bother him a bit; he supposed because we were two of a trade. He told me I was the only literary person with whom he could associate at all.

It is not difficult to picture them; the small, sturdy, bespectacled Kipling at his desk; the tall, bearded, robust Haggard in a chair nearby, notebook on knee (as likely as not), jotting down ideas for future novels. Both of them at ease and contented, in perfect harmony. Peering through the half-open door of that study, we have been given a glimpse of two celebrated authors at work; let us close it gently again, and leave them to their privacy and peace.

NOTE: Unpublished material by Kipling and Haggard is quoted from the original letters and notebooks in my collection; it is printed here with the gracious permission of the Haggard and Kipling families.—J. E. S.

The "Presentation" *Paradise Lost*

By JAMES THORPE

ONLY one author-presentation copy of *Paradise Lost* is recorded. Although well known, either it has never before been sufficiently examined or the results of previous examinations have been stated with a remarkable lack of candor. In short, there are reasons for a bibliographer to have serious doubts about the authenticity of the inscriptions which have allowed it to pass as a presentation copy with an inscription in Milton's hand.

The descriptions of this copy which have been rendered in the course of its recorded history are an interesting study in accretion. That history commences in 1896 with lot 573 of "A Portion of the Library of a Collector," which was sold by Sotheby, Wilkinson, and Hodge on March 19-21, 1896. After describing the copy as a first edition of *Paradise Lost,* the Sotheby catalogue adds the following information about the inscriptions:

> **A MOST IMPORTANT AND INTERESTING COPY, having on the first flyleaf, "For my loving ffriend Mr. Francis Rea Booke binder in Worcestershire," and on the next flyleaf, "Presented unto me by the Author to whom I gave 2 doubl Souveranges."

Quaritch bought the book for £85.

Less than a year later this copy was again sold at auction by Sotheby, Wilkinson, and Hodge. It was included as lot 1032 of "Libraries Belonging to Several Gentlemen," which were dispersed on February 22-26, 1897. At that sale Maggs bought it for £80. Although I have not examined the catalogue of that sale, it should be safe to assume that the description is virtually identical with that of the previous year, because both entries in *Book-Prices Current* (X[1896], p. 211 and XI[1897], p. 122) quote the two inscriptions with substantially the same comment as that quoted above from the 1896 sale catalogue.

The copy then passed into the library of Robert Hoe. The auction record is concluded with its sale on May 2, 1911, in the dispersal of the Hoe Library. In the *Catalogue of the Library of Robert Hoe* (I, lot 2294) the two inscriptions are again quoted, after the simple remark that "the following inscriptions are on the first two fly-leaves." This time the copy fetched $1,750, more than four times its previous record at auction; it was bought by Walter M. Hill of Chicago.

It should be noted that this copy was not *explicitly* described as a presentation copy in the catalogues or annual auction records through the time of the Hoe sale in 1911. Similarly, when Luther S. Livingston cited this copy in 1905 in his *Auction Prices of Books* (III, p. 223), he simply quoted the inscriptions and stated that they appeared on the flyleaves. Perhaps this is a fine distinction to make, as the reader would no doubt assume (as he was, in the case of the sales catalogues, probably expected to assume), that he was dealing with a genuine author's presentation copy of *Paradise Lost*.

No one of the several people who have written about this copy since the Hoe sale has had an opportunity to examine it, for it was lost to sight in 1911. The references to it since that time show various degrees of invention. The entry in *American Book-Prices Current* for 1911 (XVII, p. 476) describes it as a "presentation copy to Francis Rea from Milton, with inscription on fly-leaf, also with inscription by Rea." Thus it became, for the first time, explicitly a "presentation copy." In 1921, Seymour de Ricci referred to it in *The Book Collector's Guide* (p. 412) as a "presentation copy to Francis Rea, with Milton's autograph." And so it became not only a presentation copy, but one with an inscription in Milton's own handwriting, the possibility that it was the work of an amanuensis being disregarded. In 1938 it was confidently included in the definitive Columbia edition of Milton's works (XVIII, pp. 270, 549) among the Milton presentation copies. The first inscription is quoted in the section on Book Inscriptions, which includes "only such presentation inscriptions as involved original composition by Milton"; it is headed, *"From a copy of Paradise Lost, given to Francis Rea, 1667."* This entry not only recognizes the copy as a presentation with an inscription by Milton but also assigns an exact date to the gift. Thus, without benefit of examination, descriptions of this copy changed from a bare (and perhaps equivocal) statement of fact in an auction catalogue to a more elaborate set of assumptions presented as fact in a work of high scholarship.

Only Professor J. Milton French had a qualm about the inscriptions. He quoted them in his important essay on "The Autographs of John Milton" in the *Journal of English Literary History* for 1937; but when he attempted to trace the copy which contained the inscriptions in order to examine them, he failed. The buyer at the Hoe sale, Walter M. Hill, had "no recollection or record of its purchase or sale." Professor French and the bibliographical world were left with little alternative but to accept the unique presentation *Paradise Lost* as genuine. Such a position had the weight of tradition (if not examination) in its favor.

Now, thirty-seven years after the Hoe sale, the presentation *Paradise Lost* has turned up in the Princeton University Library. The blank interval in its history can be easily filled in. The late Cyrus H. McCormick obtained the book from Hill in 1911; in fact, it appears from the McCormick records that Hill had simply been acting as McCormick's agent when he bid this book in for $1,750. Since 1911 it has remained inconspicuously in the McCormick Collection, which was recently presented to Princeton by Mr. McCormick's widow.

The "presentation" *Paradise Lost* is an excellent example of the first edition, with the second 1667 title page. It is large and clean; the only faults are a few very small marginal tears so skilfully repaired as to be almost indiscernible. This copy includes the 1669 printing of the preliminary leaves between the title page and the text ("The

Printer to the Reader," Milton's prose arguments for the ten books, Milton's note on "The Verse," and a page of errata); it has the first printing of signatures Z and Vv (the two that were reprinted in 1669); and it has a normal assortment of states in the other signatures. If one accepts Professor Harris F. Fletcher's logical theory of the method of publication of *Paradise Lost* (as set forth in the introduction to the second volume of his edition of *John Milton's Complete Poetical Works*, 1945), this copy appears to be one of that last lot of a hundred or so which Samuel Simmons bound up in April 1669 out of the remaining sheets, among which he found and used some of the second 1667 title pages; four other similar copies are recorded.

More important for our present purposes, this copy has three leaves preliminary to the title page. The first two bear the advertised inscriptions, and on the third has been skilfully affixed the very rare smaller engraving of Milton by T. Phinn after Faithorne (Number 55 in the Grolier *Catalogue of an Exhibition Commemorative of the Tercentenary of the Birth of John Milton 1608-1908*). Since the inscriptions are not quoted altogether correctly in the sales catalogues referred to earlier (nor, of course, in the annual auction records, the Columbia Milton, or the other references to this copy, all of which are based on the catalogue descriptions), they must be again transcribed. This is the inscription that appears on the first leaf: "For | My loving ffriend M^r | Francis Rea Booke- | binder in Worcester | these | [flourishes] |."

The "Presentation" *Paradise Lost* 361

The second leaf has the following inscription: "Presented vnto me by the | Author to whome I gave | 2 doubl souverayns |." If we accept these inscriptions at their face value, the first is by Milton and the second by Francis Rea. (It is surprising that no one of the modern critics of Milton has capitalized on these inscriptions and constructed a new myth about Milton's niggardliness. If a passing remark by Keats, or a brief but deliberate comment by Blake, was worth a chapter in the hands of Mr. Middleton Murry, surely some basis could be found here for defamation.)

The most serious error in the previous transcriptions of these inscriptions is the incorrect reading of "Worcestershire" for "Worcester | these." I must confess at the outset that the correct reading of the presentation formula seems to me less suggestive of a copy of *Paradise Lost* than it does of a bundle of broadsides or a basket of fresh eggs.

An examination of these inscriptions may begin with some observations on the chain lines of the preliminary leaves. Several remarkable features immediately become apparent. The first leaf presents an awkward face consisting of both transverse and vertical chain lines. The chain lines of the leaf at large (and of the book as a whole, of course) are transverse. That portion of the leaf on which the "Milton" inscription is written—a section which measures about two inches by three inches—has vertical chain lines. When we look a little more closely, we find that this section has been very skilfully inserted into the leaf; the papers are similar, and the workmanship highly expert. The second leaf—which bears the inscription of the recipient—is curious in a rather different way. Its chain lines are vertical throughout. The chain lines of the third preliminary leaf are in the normal transverse position. This evidence of the chain lines might suggest even to the least suspicious nature that the authenticity of the inscriptions is open to question. The evidence does not totally disprove the claims put forward for them, however. The inserted section of the first leaf could possibly be a restoration of a damaged leaf or of an inscription originally on an endpaper. Furthermore, it is dangerous to generalize categorically on the position of chain lines in the preliminary leaves of a book that was bound up in as many different ways and at as many different times as was the first edition of *Paradise Lost*.

An examination of the watermarks discloses further peculiarities. The small section inserted in the first leaf bears no watermark, but its leaf and the other two leaves preliminary to the title page all bear watermarks. This fact in itself suggests that there is something abnormal about these leaves, that at least they were not drawn from the same sheet. The watermark of the first preliminary leaf is in normal quarto position, centered in the inner margin; the lower half of the mark is visible, but a small portion of the bottom of the mark has been removed by the insert. It appears to be the arms of France and Navarre, Heawood's Number 4 ("Papers Used in England After 1600," *The Library*, 1930-1931), Churchill's Number 308 (*Watermarks in Paper...*, 1935). The watermark of the second leaf is horizontally centered in the lower section of the leaf. I do not recognize it in the usual guides to watermarks. Although it cannot be exactly described, it resembles slightly a rounded shield (or shell) with irregular markings, and bears a trifling similarity, in outward form only, to Churchill's Number 301 upside down. The watermark of the third leaf occurs at the outer margin and appears to be the top fourth of the arms of France and Navarre noted above. (It is a curious coincidence—though apparently nothing more than a coincidence—that the paper of the first and third preliminary leaves bears the same watermark as that of the paper used for the fourth edition of *Paradise Lost*, published in 1688 by Bentley and Tonson.) Professor Fletcher, in the second volume of his edition of *Milton's Poetical Works*, records a careful investigation of the watermarks in over fifty copies of the first edition of *Paradise Lost*.

He has classified, catalogued, reproduced, and discussed the marks. The watermarks of these three preliminary leaves are strikingly dissimilar to all of the marks which he has noted. Furthermore, it is almost certain from the position of the watermarks that these three leaves were not originally bound up with this copy. The position of the mark on the second leaf suggests that that leaf was removed from a folio and cut down to quarto size. Since the authenticity of these inscriptions is largely dependent on the support which one gives to the other, it seems important to emphasize that the two inscribed leaves do not appear to go together; this is manifest from their different watermarks and from the different positions of chain lines and watermarks. From the evidence so far presented we may, I think, assert at least that the inscribed leaves were not originally a part of this copy. Two bare but unlikely possibilities remain which could render them of significance. One is that the leaves were haphazardly added in a rebinding of the copy during the five years between its issue and Milton's death, with the first leaf later restored. The other possibility is that they were somehow originally connected with another work of Milton's published during his lifetime and later transferred to this copy.

We may finally turn to a consideration of the handwriting. The "Milton" inscription is done in a neat and conventional seventeenth-century hand. Anyone who has seen Milton's tortured attempts at writing after about 1653 or 1654 (when he had become totally blind) would immediately deny that Milton could have written this inscription in or after 1667. Milton could not keep even his signature on a straight line; certainly he could not have written this careful and regular five-line inscription, complete with flourishes, after 1654. Furthermore, a critical comparison of this sample with all of Milton's genuine handwriting makes it clear that this inscription is unlike Milton's writing at any time, before or after his blindness. This statement may be made in complete confidence. However, his various amanuenses still remain to be reckoned with. If the inscription were written by one of Milton's amanuenses, it might have some significance. Through the kindness of my friend, Professor Maurice Kelley, I have been able to compare this inscription with his complete set of samples of the handwriting of all of the recognized amanuenses. No similarity was noticed in any of those comparisons. For these reasons, there seems to be no basis for connecting the "Milton" inscription with Milton in any way. Nothing can be said about the handwriting on the second leaf, that ascribed to Francis Rea, as samples of his writing seem not to have survived. From the little that is known of him as a bookseller and bookbinder, however, he seems to have had no connection with Milton other than that suggested by these attributed inscriptions.

It would certainly be a more pleasant task to be able to discover another presentation copy of *Paradise Lost* than to suggest the removal of the unique one from the rolls. However, from the bibliographical evidence at hand it must be concluded that this copy of *Paradise Lost* was not presented by Milton to Francis Rea or to anyone else and that the preliminary apparatus (which cannot be connected with this copy nor with *Paradise Lost* in general nor with Milton at all) was carefully fabricated sometime before 1896 and has heretofore been accepted as genuine.

It would be interesting to know who prepared and assembled the preliminary leaves and connected them with this copy. The book has obviously undergone no change since it was rebound. The binding is red levant morocco with scroll tooling, narrow inside dentelles, and gilt edges. It is an excellent example of the work of Francis Bedford, to whom it is ascribed in the 1896 auction catalogue. The material used strongly suggests that it is a sample of his later work, when he had turned from tree calf to morocco. But because of the extremely long span of Bedford's work—he was active virtually up to the time of his death at the age of eighty-four—that suggestion is not very helpful in establishing its date with any preciseness. One might say only that the binding dates somewhere between 1855 and 1880. As W. Y. Fletcher observed in his *DNB* account of Bedford (which is an excellent sketch and more detailed than the remarks on Bedford in his *Bookbinding in England and France*): "Bedford appreciated tall copies, and a book never came from his hands shorn of its margins. He was also a very skilful mender of damaged leaves." It was probably Bedford who repaired those few torn margins in this copy so carefully that they can be identified only upon very close examination. He possessed exactly the kind of knowledge and skill (which had been rare before him) to be able to insert the section containing the "Milton" inscription into the first leaf and otherwise to prepare the preliminary apparatus for binding.

Who commissioned the fabrication that resulted in a unique presentation *Paradise Lost*? Unfortunately, I cannot trace the history of the copy before 1896. Sotheby & Company has reported as follows: "We find it impossible, for reasons of space, to preserve our old ledgers and similar records, and we have now no private records regarding the ownership of Lots sold as far back as 1896." Therefore, for a definite conclusion as to who was really responsible for the fabrication, "the result seems to be" (as Boswell said of Richard Savage's parentage) "that the world must vibrate in a state of uncertainty as to what was the truth."

To commemorate the 150th
anniversary of lithography, *The New Colophon* presents
a contemporary example of the art

The discovery of another printing surface was not entirely an accident. The young actor, composer, poet, law student, who contributed lithography to the world knew considerable about the two printing surfaces already in use at the end of the eighteenth century, and he was experimenting with the printing of music. A happy incident was the chance availability in his home at Munich of a stone with unusual qualities, a stone with an affinity for both oil and water, two liquids that will not cohere.

Up to the late 1790's, when Alois Senefelder began to experiment, all printing was produced from a physical surface, either relief or intaglio. These two surfaces differ mainly in the inking. To print from the relief surface, the outward or projecting part is inked; while quite to the reverse, to print from the intaglio, ink is rubbed into the crevices, the cuts below the surface. The relief surface of the intaglio plate is kept clean of ink.

Inasmuch as the lithograph is made possible by chemical action, it is neither relief nor intaglio, but planographic. It became the third of the surfaces for printing or manifolding. To apply a design or composition to a lithograph stone no cutting is necessary; the artist draws on the sensitive stone with a greasy crayon, and before the stone is inked for printing it is thoroughly moistened with water. The grease of the crayon resists the water, but will hold the printing ink that the wet part of the stone will not hold. This, briefly, is the principle of lithography.

Although Senefelder had perfected the new method of printing by 1798, nearly two decades passed before the lithograph was in any general practice, and the first American lithograph was made in 1818.

The lithograph continues to be a very popular medium in America for artist's expression, perhaps for the reason that it is the most autographic and direct of all the graphic art techniques.

When steam and then electric power came, in the nineteenth century, other machines were developed for rapid printing. Today, only artist's proofs, such as the one here inserted, continue to be produced on the original hand presses. In the printing of this lithograph, the stone was re-inked by hand roller for each impression, just as Senefelder developed the process. Benton Spruance of Philadelphia, who was commissioned to make the sesquicentennial print for The New Colophon, received the first prize for a lithograph at the Sixth National Exhibition of Prints this year, at the Library of Congress. The sketch for the print was made at Newtown, Bucks County, Pennsylvania. The press work on the insert was done by Theodore Cuno in Philadelphia. The paper is all rag, Italian made. Each proof is signed by the artist.

ELMER ADLER

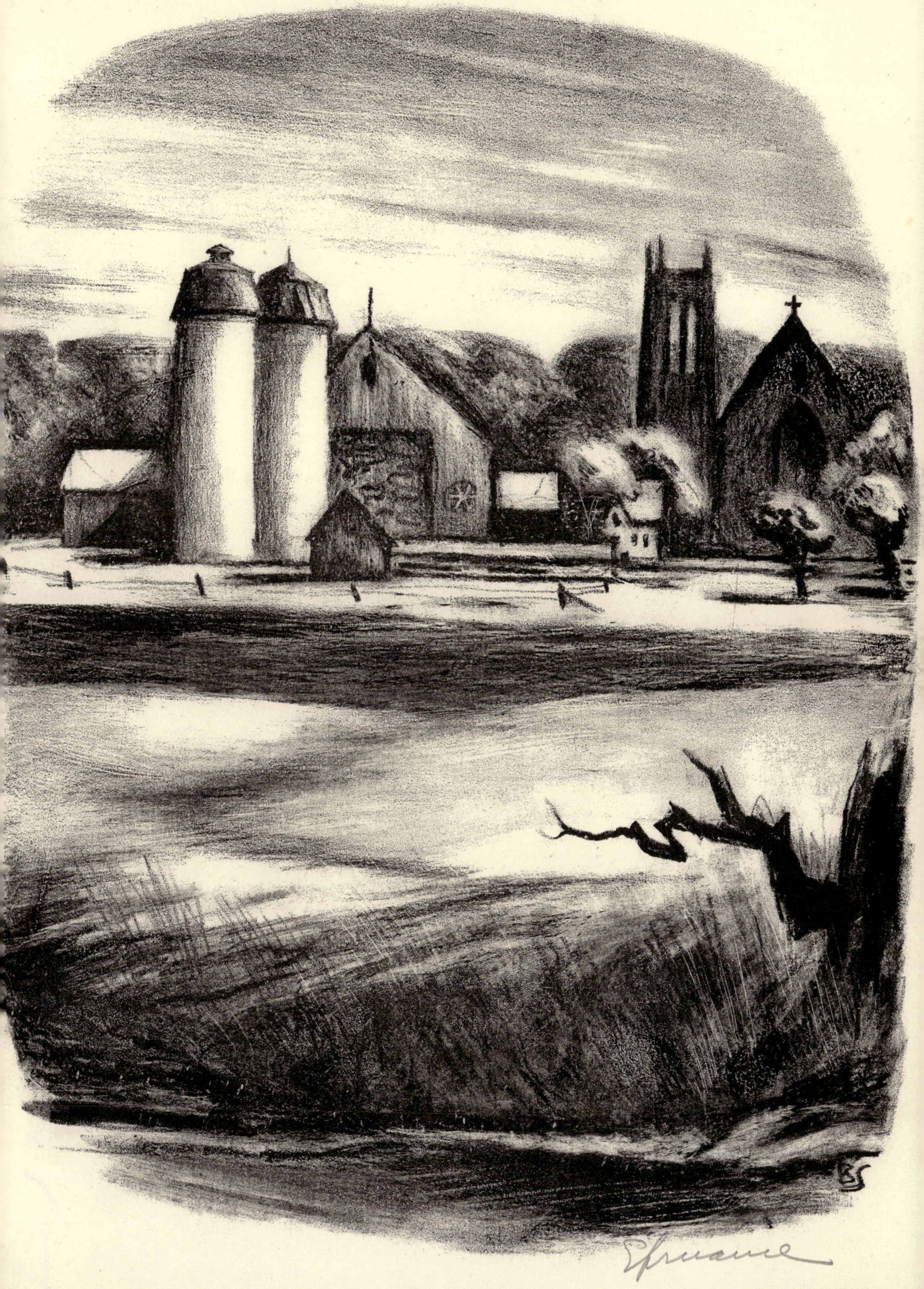

Mr. THOREAU WRITES A BOOK

By JAMES PLAYSTED WOOD

IN 1848 a short, strong-minded young man of aloof nature, independent spirit, and a long Emersonian nose (through which, as Henry Thoreau told his neighbors in a lyceum talk[1] early in the year, he preferred to breathe after his own fashion) was living once more in his native Concord village. From July 4, 1845, to September 6, 1847, he had lived alone in the one-room house he had built at Walden Pond on its outskirts.

At Walden, Thoreau had written, from the records in his Journal, a narrative of the voyage from Concord, Massachusetts, almost to Concord in New Hampshire which he and his brother John, who died in 1842, had taken from August 31 to September 13, 1839. Emerson's "wise young neighbors," as he called them in noting the excursion in his own Journal, had fashioned their boat, the Musketaquid, themselves, even contriving sails which would serve as a tent at night.[2] When he left Walden, Thoreau brought the manuscript narrative back with him to the Emerson household, where, for the second time, he was to stay while Emerson was abroad. Throughout 1848 he was working intently getting what was to be his first book ready for publication.

The projected book had been known and talked about in Concord

[1] Thoreau delivered "Civil Disobedience" before the Concord Lyceum in January, 1848. It was first published as "Resistance to Civil Government" in Elizabeth Peabody's *Aesthetic Papers* in 1849.
[2] Nathaniel Hawthorne bought the Musketaquid in 1843 when Thoreau went to Staten Island to tutor William Emerson's children. He describes Thoreau's delivery of the boat in one of the happiest passages of the *American Note-Books*.

at least since the summer of 1846. Whimsical Ellery Channing, Thoreau's walking companion and closest friend as well as his first biographer, disparaged, but Emerson was enthusiastic. In one of the first known notices of its existence, he wrote Charles King Newcomb, July 16, 1846, that the manuscript of Thoreau's *Excursion on the Concord and Merrimack Rivers* would appear as a book "if Wiley and Putnam smile. He read me some of it under an oak on the river the other afternoon and invigorated me."[3] Bronson Alcott was even more delighted. "This evening I pass with Thoreau at his hermitage on Walden," Alcott wrote, March 16, 1847, "and he reads me some passages from his manuscript entitled 'A Week on the Concord and Merrimac Rivers.' The book is purely American, fragrant with the life of New England woods and streams, and could have been written nowhere else. Especially am I touched by his sufficiency and soundness, his aboriginal vigor—as if a man had once come into Nature who knew what Nature meant him to do with her; Virgil and White of Selborne, and Izaak Walton, and Yankee settler, all in one. I came home at midnight through the snowy woodpaths, and slept with the pleasing dream that the press would give me two books to be proud of,—Emerson's *Poems* and Thoreau's *Week*."[4]

Emerson had long been trying to find a publisher for his young friend's book. As early as March 12, 1847, he wrote Evert Duyckinck in New York that "Mr. Henry Thoreau of this town has just completed a book of extraordinary merit. . . . It will be as attractive to lovers of nature . . . as Isaak Walton. It will be attractive to scholars for its excellent literature and to all thoughtful persons for its originality and soundness. It is really a book of the results of the studies of years." Emerson said he had advised Thoreau that his best course would be to send the book to Duyckinck to be printed by Wiley and Putnam, "that it may have a good edition and wide publishing." He was sure that Thoreau, who had not yet submitted the manuscript to any pub-

---

[3] *The Letters of Ralph Waldo Emerson*, edited by Ralph S. Rusk, New York, 1939, Vol. III, p. 339.

[4] *The Journals of Bronson Alcott*, selected and edited by Odell Shepard, Boston 1938, pp. 213-215. Alcott used the spelling "Merrimac." Thoreau preferred the older "Merrimack."

lisher, would readily send it at once for his perusal.[5] Duyckinck replied only that he would be glad to read the manuscript and offer his advice.

In August, 1847, Emerson tried through W. H. Furness, the Unitarian preacher who had been his schoolmate in Boston, to obtain a Philadelphia publisher for the *Week,* writing, "Thoreau is mainly bent on having it printed in a cheap form for wide circulation." Furness reported, August 16, 1847, that a new publisher named Moore desired to see the manuscript. A month later, September 19, 1847, he wrote that Carey and Hart could not undertake the book. No other Philadelphia house leaped at the chance to publish Thoreau's first book; nor did Harper's or the other New York publishers whose attention was solicited through William Emerson.

Thirty-year-old Thoreau was virtually unknown beyond Concord. He had written prose or verse for almost every issue of the *Dial,* while helping Margaret Fuller and Emerson bring out the Transcendentalist magazine which had lapsed in 1844, but his article on Carlyle, which Horace Greeley had managed to get into *Graham's,* was, in 1847, as yet his only appearance as an author before the general reading public.[6]

Wiley and Putnam and Harper's in New York, Munroe and Crosby and Nichols in Boston and Cambridge, all rejected the *Week,* though as Thoreau, November 14, 1847, wrote ironically to Emerson, who was now in England, all were quite willing to print it at his expense.[7] The aspiring author began to lose confidence in his work, but tried to hide his disappointment by saying in the same letter: "For the last month or two I have forgotten it.... For the present I am indifferent."

Emerson would allow no such pique and despondency. "I am not of the opinion your book should be delayed a month," he urged in reply. "I should print it at once, nor do I think you would incur any

---
[5] Rusk, *op. cit.,* Vol. III, p. 384.
[6] "Thomas Carlyle and his Works," *Graham's Magazine,* March and April, 1847.
[7] *Familiar Letters of H. D. Thoreau,* edited with an introduction and notes by F. B. Sanborn, Boston, 1894, p. 166.

risk in doing so that you cannot well afford. It is certain to have readers and debtors, here as well as there."[8] Emerson, who was appreciatively relearning in England the value of authorship as a means to recognition, was anxious for Thoreau to arrive. In a letter to his wife he urged Lidian, whose influence over Thoreau he knew was considerable, not to let him delay another day in getting out his book.[9]

The depressing effect of numerous rejections and continued delay was proving no stimulus to Thoreau, who wrote as much to Elliot Cabot. He did not like his book well enough to pay for its printing. At least such was his wry declaration. What he did not like was the idea of going into debt. He liked the *Week* well enough, he admitted, to mend it.

He was enlarging as well as mending. He put some of his lecture material into the manuscript, as well as poems and prose essays which he had used in the *Dial*. Allen lists fifteen *Dial* items which Thoreau transferred into his book manuscript.[10] In January, 1848, he read to Alcott, who continued a firm and discerning admirer of both Thoreau and his book, the emotion-charged essay on "Friendship" which he had just written. Someone once remarked that Emerson's writing on the subject pales by comparison with Thoreau's. Henry Seidel Canby has conjectured that love, not friendship, was its real subject, and that it was of his emotions toward Lidian Emerson that Thoreau wrote.[11] Thoreau inserted the essay, of whose worth he must have been well aware, into the Wednesday chapter of the *Week*. He thought that well of his book.

Horace Greeley was insisting from New York that Thoreau write more articles for magazine publication. Greeley believed in magazines. He had edited and loved his *New-Yorker* before his *Tribune* days. "Though you may write with an angel's pen yet your work will have no mercantile value unless you are known as an author," he wrote

---

[8] Sanborn, *op. cit.*, p. 187.

[9] Rusk, *op. cit.*, Vol. IV, p. 16.

[10] *A Bibliography of Henry David Thoreau*, compiled by Francis H. Allen, Boston and New York, 1908, pp. 64-68.

[11] Canby, *Thoreau*, New York, 1939.

Thoreau. "Emerson would be twice as well known if he had written for the magazines a little just to let common people know of his existence."[12]

But Thoreau was too busy on the *Week*. Perhaps later, he told Greeley, he would do the shorter articles Greeley wanted. "My book grows in bulk as I work on it!" he exulted. Thoreau never got around to the short articles, though it was Greeley who, acting virtually as Thoreau's literary agent, saw to the publication of "Ktaadn" in Sartain's *Union Magazine* in the issues of July, August, September, and October, 1848, and later arranged for partial publication of "Cape Cod" and "A Yankee in Canada" in *Putnam's Magazine* which George William Curtis was editing.

The efforts of Thoreau's friends to secure a publisher for his book continued; and they continued to fail. Thoreau was discouraged. He would not, he insisted, undertake the risk himself. Then something obviously happened which made him change his mind. What did happen is conjecture merely. He came to recognize the soundness of the more experienced Emerson's advice, or Greeley's warnings took effect, or—and more likely—his young man's pride in his work, imaginings of the joy of seeing his work between hard covers, and some of his desperate stubbornness combined to make him more daring. He arranged with James Munroe of Boston to publish the book at the author's expense. One wonders what the exact financial details of the agreement were.[13] Thoreau wrote down later an exact enough account of their result.

Page proofs of the *Week* were in Thoreau's hands before the end of the year. He went over them meticulously, making over a thousand corrections. One resulted in the well-known error on page 396 of the published book. Thoreau asked for more space and the printer obliged but failed to carry three lines over to the next page. The copyright date in the page proofs is 1848, showing how narrowly Thoreau escaped publication in the same year that was the *annus mirabilis* of his most

---

[12] Quoted by Henry Luther Stoddard in *Horace Greeley, Printer, Editor, Crusader*, New York, 1946, p. 279.

[13] Obviously, one doesn't know.

unfriendly critic, James Russell Lowell, who got out *Poems: Second Series, The Biglow Papers, The Vision of Sir Launfal,* and *A Fable for Critics,* all under an 1848 date. In 1848 the *Week* would have had to compete too with *Jane Eyre, Wuthering Heights, The Tenant of Wildfell Hall, Vanity Fair,* and John Quincy Adams' *Poems of Religion and Society.*[14] Instead the *Week* came out in 1849 with Parkman's *The Oregon Trail* for decent contemporary.

Actual publication was nearing when Emerson wrote Ellen Randall, May 22, 1849: "My friend Thoreau is shortly to publish a book ... which, I think, will win the best readers abroad and at home."[15] Alcott recorded receipt of his copy four days later. "Today comes Henry Thoreau to town and gives me a copy of his book, just published, by James Munroe & Co., entitled 'A Week on the Concord and Merrimack Rivers.'—12mo. pp. 413. An American book worthy to stand beside Emerson's Essays on my shelves."[16] Alcott read the book all the next day and found it good. It is pleasant to know that this genuinely appreciative critic of the manuscript felt his early estimates justified.

May 26, 1849, was publication date. At least, Thoreau wrote Harrison Blake on August 10, 1849, that he had directed a copy to be sent him from Munroe's shop on that date, "before a copy had been sold." According to the Boston *Daily Advertiser,* cited by Rusk, it was published on May 30, 1849.[17]

The book resembled the Ticknor and Fields "little brown books," having the same sober brown boards stamped with an intricate floral design. A copy of the first edition in the New York Public Library is inscribed, in an elegant, shaded hand, "Editor of Literary World with Respects of the Publishers." The editor of the *Literary World* was, of course, Evert Duyckinck. The copy bears manuscript corrections "possibly by Thoreau"—they were the corrections he made later in copies he sold at Concord. On page 120 "work" is changed to "wash,"

---

[14] *Poems of Religion and Society* did not make the best seller list in 1848. Neither did Ned Buntline's *Mysteries and Miseries of New York,* though it attracted much attention. The others, excepting Anne Brontë's novel, did.

[15] Rusk, *op. cit.,* Vol. IV, pp. 145-146.

[16] Shepard, *op. cit.,* p. 209.

[17] Rusk, *op. cit.,* Vol. IV, footnote, p. 151.

and on page 139 "experience" is changed to "expediency." "Experience" was changed to "expedience" on page 139 in the copy which Thoreau gave Hawthorne. In all the copies that Thoreau personally sold or gave away he wrote in the three lines missing at the foot of page 396.

Emerson's efforts on behalf of Thoreau and his first book did not cease with its publication. Theodore Parker, meaning to be humorous, asked Emerson, who was now at home again in Concord, to review the *Week* for his *Massachusetts Quarterly Review*. Parker, who considered Thoreau merely an affected imitator of Emerson, practically said as much in his letter. Emerson seriously replied, June 11, 1849, "I am not the man to write the notice of Thoreau's book. I am of the same clan and parish. You must give it to a good foreigner. E. P. Whipple has good literary insulation and is a superior critic.[18] Will he not try his hand on this? If not he, will not Starr King? If not the one or the other, why not send to the New Yorkers, to Henry James, Parke Godwin, or C. Dana? The book has rare claims, & we must have an American claim and ensign marked on it before it goes abroad for English opinions."[19]

It was one of the major misfortunes of Thoreau's career that Parker gave the *Week* for review to none of these, but to James Russell Lowell, who had been prejudiced against Thoreau from his undergraduate days at Harvard. Rusticating in Concord during his senior year, the young Cambridge sophisticate had written derisively: "I met Thoreau last night, and it is exquisitely amusing to see how he imitates Emerson's tone and manner. With my eyes shut, I shouldn't know them apart."[20] Lowell's eyes were never opened where Thoreau was concerned. He had pilloried Thoreau in *A Fable for Critics* in 1848:

> *There comes—, for instance; to see him's rare sport,*
> *Tread in Emerson's tracks with legs painfully short;*
> *How he jumps, how he strains, and gets red in the face*
> *To keep step with the mystagogue's natural pace!*

---

[18] The two volumes of Whipple's *Essays and Reviews* appeared in 1848.
[19] Rusk, *op. cit.*, Vol. IV, p. 151.
[20] *Letters of James Russell Lowell*, edited by Charles Eliot Norton, New York, 1894, Vol. I, p. 27. Norton did not quote this Lowell letter in full nor say to whom it was written.

He follows as close as a stick to a rocket,
His fingers exploring his prophet's each pocket.
Fie, for shame, brother bard! With good fruit of your own
Can't you let neighbor Emerson's orchards alone?

Lowell's review of *A Week on the Concord and Merrimack Rivers* in the *Massachusetts Quarterly* for December, 1849, was flippant, clever, and patronizing. He managed two generous remarks: "It's being a book at all is a happy fortuity"—"the language has a purity like wine grown colorless with age." For the rest, he found fault with Thoreau's poetry in the book and attacked what he would, of course, call its "worsification"; with Thoreau's talk of Oriental philosophy, with the numerous digressions in the narrative; and particularly with what he saw as Thoreau's exaggerated belief in the importance of his own ideas.

Compared with Lowell's vicious attack in *My Study Windows* in 1865, an essay compact of disparagement and disdain,[21] his 1849 review was mild, yet it did the *Week* no good. A review by George Ripley, late of Brook Farm, in *The New-York Daily Tribune*, June 13, 1849, did further damage. Though Ripley pointed to virtues in the *Week*, he was horrified by Thoreau's assertion that he considered the Sacred Books of the Brahmins in no way inferior to the Christian Bible. Thoreau, Ripley exclaimed, evidently did not know his Bible very well. He should have made himself thoroughly familiar with it before "uttering opinions calculated to pain many readers, not to speak of those who will be utterly repelled by them. Can that which Milton and Newton so profoundly reverenced (and they had studied it thoroughly) be wisely turned off by a youth as unworthy of even consid-

---

[21] In *My Study Windows* Lowell described Thoreau as uncouth, insincere, humorless, a shantyman, a pompous rustic, conceited, and a hypocritical weakling with a morbid mind. A nicely written passage reads: "Was he indolent, he finds none of the activities which attract or employ the rest of mankind worthy of him. Was he wanting in the qualities that make success, it is success that is contemptible, and not himself that lacks persistency and purpose. Was he poor, money was an unmixed evil. Did his life seem a selfish one, he condemns doing good as one of the weakest of superstitions. To be of use was with him the most killing bait of the wily tempter Uselessness. He had no faculty of generalization outside himself, or at least no experience which would supply the material of such, and he makes his own whim the law, his own range the horizon of the universe. He condemns a world, the hollowness of whose satisfactions he had never had the means of testing, and we recognize Apemantus behind the mask of Timon." Though Lowell makes gestures toward the charitable, the entire essay is done in the same vein of high dislike.

eration? Mr. Thoreau's treatment of the subject seems revolting alike to good sense and good taste."

As a publishing venture, *A Week on the Concord and Merrimack Rivers* was a dismal and disheartening failure. Thoreau had hoped to let the world know the story of his voyage with John, and to tell the world of the thoughts and emotions he had penned in peaceful days at Walden when the sun danced on the surface of the pond or when the woods between him and the village were deep in snow, and the ice in Walden was thick and clear. Instead, he scarcely informed his neighbors, who knew both story and ideas anyway.

More than four years after its publication only two hundred and ninety-four copies of the *Week* had been distributed, and of this number seventy-five had been given away. October 28, 1853, Munroe returned the remaining seven hundred and six copies of the edition of one thousand to their author, and Thoreau carefully entered in what has become one of the best known passages of his Journal: "I have now a library of nearly nine hundred volumes, over seven hundred of which I wrote myself. Is it not well that the author should behold the fruits of his labor?" Real courage and a painful bravado are mixed in his further remark. "Nevertheless, in spite of the result, sitting here beside the inert mass of my works, I take up my pen tonight to record what thoughts or experience I may have had, with as much satisfaction as ever. Indeed, I believe that this result is more inspiring and better for me than if a thousand had bought my wares. It affects my privacy less and leaves me freer."

Thoreau had still not paid fully for the publication of the *Week*. At one time, says Alcott, he considered speculating in cranberries to help pay his debt. Instead he surveyed and made pencils. When he settled finally with Munroe, November 28, 1853, he noted that he had paid the publisher $290 directly, and to repay $100 he had borrowed elsewhere to guarantee the book's publication he was forced, as he said, to manufacture a thousand dollars' worth of pencils and sell them at sacrifice prices.

Twelve copies of the book Thoreau placed with Munroe, at the time of the settlement, for the publisher to sell. October 18, 1854, he left an equal number for sale with Fields. Thoreau managed to sell a few copies, at $1.25 each, from his own stock, but very few. This was the price he quoted C. H. Green in a letter, January 18, 1856, and this was the price paid him by Sarah Sanborn in 1855.

April 30, 1855, Thoreau wrote Munroe asking if it were not time to republish *A Week on the Concord and Merrimack Rivers,* saying that he had two hundred and fifty bound copies and four hundred and fifty in sheets. It was not until 1862, however, the year of Thoreau's death, that Ticknor and Fields brought out a second edition. Actually, this second edition was the rebound sheets of the first. It is a curiosity in that the publishers forgot to remove the 1849 announcement on a page at the back that *Walden* would "soon be published." *Walden* had appeared in 1854. Ticknor and Fields issued a revised edition of the *Week* in 1868. Since then there have been few editions, none of them exceptional.

New editions of *Walden* appear now almost annually. Given Thoreau's experience with *A Week on the Concord and Merrimack Rivers,* it is a wonder there was ever a first of *Walden.*

Robert Waldegrave and the Pirates of Dunkirk

By CURT F. BÜHLER

ROBERT Waldegrave[1] was apprenticed as a printer to the stationer William Griffith in London on June 24, 1568, and ten years later his first entry appears in the Register of the Stationer's Company. Subsequently he was attracted to the Puritan movement, and agitated against the privileged printers. On at least two occasions he was thrown into prison for printing unlicensed books or Puritan tracts; and in 1588 his press and types were seized and defaced. Following this seizure, Waldegrave began his peripatetic career, printing several of the Martin Marprelate tracts in various places of refuge, and always keeping just one step ahead of the pursuivants of the church and of the Company of Stationers.

Eventually Waldegrave fled to Scotland, apparently by way of Rochelle, where he may have printed other Puritan tracts. In Edinburgh, he became an almost immediate success, for he was appointed printer to the King (James VI) on October 9, 1590, and from that date to James's succession to the throne of England (March 24, 1603) he printed over a hundred books. He apparently followed James to London, for on June 11, 1603, a book was entered to him in the Station-

[1] For further particulars of Waldegrave's career, see *A Dictionary of Printers and Booksellers in England, Scotland, and Ireland . . . 1557-1640*, London, 1910, pp. 277-279; Ronald B. McKerrow, *Printers' & Publishers' Devices in England & Scotland,* London, 1913, p. 183; Robert Dickson and John P. Edmond, *Annals of Scottish Printing,* Cambridge, 1890, pp. 394-474; Edward Arber, *An Introductory Sketch to the Martin Marprelate Controversy,* London, 1879; J. Dover Wilson's chapter on "Martin Marprelate" in *CHEL,* III, chapter xvii, and two other articles by the same writer: "A Date in the Marprelate Controversy," *The Library,* 2nd ser., VIII, 337-359, and "A New Tract from the Marprelate Press," *ibid.,* X, 225-240.

IACOBVS DEI GRATIA REX SCOTORVM SERENISSIMO PRINCIPI ALBERTO eadem gratia Archiduci Austriæ, Duci Brabantiæ, Burgundiæq, consanguineo et fratri nostro charissimo, Salutem et perpetuum fœlicitatis omnis incrementum. Serenissime Princeps consanguinee et frater charissime, cum anno superiore captus esset à naui Dunkerkensi subditus noster Ioannes Smelius ciuis Edinburgensis, commendatitias nostras obtinuit, quibus faciliorem ad Ser.tem vestram aditum inueniret, faciliusq, impetraret vt bona tam ipsi quam alijs subditis nostris in eadem naui à Dunkirkensibus ablata restituerentur. Verum cum singula reliquis adempta demonstrare non posset ab eorum petitione abstinuit, earum tamen mercium quas ad se pertinere docuit estimationem tanta facilitate obtinuit vt damni accepti compensationem omnino clementiæ estræ acceptam ferat. Reuerso in patriam Smelio supplices a nobis petierunt ROBERTVS WALDEGRAVIVS Typographus noster, et ROBERTVS BARNETTVS ejus gener, quorum bona (aureis mille æstimata) in eadem naui cum Smelio fuerant direpta, vt causas suas Ser.ti vestræ commendare dignaremur, quod quia ob virorum probitatem recusare non potuimus primum omnium Ser.ti vestræ gratias agimus quantas possumus maximas tam ob ipsum Smelium, quam ob singularem in nostros omnes animi propensionem: petimusque, vt eadem clementia WALDEGRAVIVM generumq, suum, eorumque procuratorem Gulielmum Morauium mercatorem Edinburgenum tractet qua erga reliquos subditos nostros hactenus est vsa. Et quia Ser.ti vestræ non leuiter deuinctos nos existimamus, dabimus operam vt nostram vicissim gratiam et fauorem vbi occasio tulerit vestris comprobemus, Deus Opt. Max. Ser.tem Vram seruet incolumen. Datæ e Regia nostra Sancruciana septimo die mensis Ianuarij Anno salutis humanæ 1603.

S V frater amantissimus

Jacobus R.

er's Register. Waldegrave died before January 5, 1604,[2] probably during December of the previous year.

In the historical collections in the Pierpont Morgan Library (Rulers of England, James I, vol. i), is a document concerning Robert Waldegrave which is of considerable interest in the history of printing in Tudor and Stuart England. It is a communication addressed, on the verso, to "Serenissimo Principi D*omi*no Alberto Dei gratia Archiduci Austriæ: Duci Brabantiæ Burgundiæq*ue* fratri et consanguineo nostro charissimo"; at the end is written in King James's own hand: *"Servus Vester* frater amantissimus Jacobus R." The body of the letter[3] reads in translation:

James, by the grace of God, King of the Scots, to the most Serene Albert,[4] by the same grace Archduke of Austria, Duke of Brabant and Burgundy, our most beloved relative and brother, greeting and continual increase of all happiness.

O most serene Prince, relative and brother most dear, when in the past year, our subject John Smaillie, a citizen of Edinburgh, was captured by a Dunkirk[5] ship, he obtained our recommendations by which means he procured easier access to your Serenity and he more easily effected that the property stolen by the Dunkirkers both from him and from those others our subjects in the same ship was restored. Nevertheless, when he was not able to identify the individual seizures from the rest, he abstained in the petition of them, though he obtained with great ease an appraisal of those wares which he stated belonged to him, so that for damage received he obtained compensation wholly through your clemency. When Smaillie returned to his homeland, Robert Waldegrave our printer and his son-in-law Robert Barnett, whose property (valued at a thousand[6] guldens) had been plundered in the same ship with Smaillie, made entreaties to us that we might deign to recommend their cases to your Serenity, which on behalf of the probity of these men we have not been able to decline, we, therefore, first give thanks—to the greatest ex-

[2] This date is given by Robert Steele, *A Bibliography of Royal Proclamations of the Tudor and Stuart Sovereigns,* Oxford, 1910, I, xxxviii.

[3] The letter came to the Morgan Library from the collection of Augustus Frederick, Duke of Sussex.

[4] Albert (1559-1621) was one of the younger sons of the Emperor Maximilian II. He served as governor of the Spanish Netherlands from February 1596 until his death.

[5] The pirates operating out of Dunkirk were a source of constant irritation to the seafaring nations. About this time the States General undertook an invasion of Flanders with the object of capturing the town and destroying this "nest of audacious pirates." Compare *Cambridge Modern History,* New York, 1907, III, 634 ff. There is a record in the Public Record Office (*Calendar of State Papers Relating to Scotland,* London, 1858, II, 796) which notes that the Dunkirkers had taken a prize ship on April 22, 1601, which may be the one referred to in this letter.

[6] According to the *Glossarium mediae et infimae latinitatis* of Du Cange, Niort, 1883-1887, I, 485, "aureus" is the normal Latin equivalent of "gulden."

tent of our power—to your Serenity both on behalf of this Smaillie and also we beg for a singular inclination of good-will towards all our [subjects], so that by the same clemency in whatever manner the procedure has hitherto been towards our remaining subjects may be extended to Waldegrave and his son-in-law and their agent William Murray, an Edinburgh merchant. And because we deem ourselves not lightly devoted to your Serenity, we will give an undertaking that (in turn) we may confirm to your [subjects] our thanks and favor when the suitable time comes about. May the Lord most powerful preserve your Serenity unharmed. Given at our Palace Holyrood, the seventh day of the month of January in the year of human salvation 1603.[7]

This letter provides us with several new details regarding the Martinist printer. The fact that Waldegrave had six children as early as 1588 and that his son Robert[8] was baptized in Edinburgh on September 26, 1596, has been common knowledge for some time. Robert Barnett is, however, new to the printer's biography. We must conclude, of course, either that Barnett had married a Waldegrave daughter or that he was Mrs. Waldegrave's brother, since *gener* usually means son-in-law, though it has also been recorded with the sense of brother-in-law. Neither John Smaillie[9] nor William Murray is to be found in the local records of their day so far as these have been published or calendared.

But much more significant than these family details are the goods valued at a thousand guldens which were stolen by the Dunkirkers. What were these goods, and how much does this figure represent in our currency? One can only surmise that the merchandise must have had something to do with Waldegrave's professional activities. It is known that he employed Dutch types[10] and, in common with other printers of the time, he probably used paper from the Netherlands; thus it may have been either paper or types, or even books printed on

[7] The date here given must be New Style, since by January, 1604, James was King of England as well as of Scotland, and Waldegrave was dead.

[8] See the *Scottish Antiquary*, IV, 174. The witnesses were the "Lord Ambassidour" and Nicoll Uddart, merchant. Robert Waldegrave, Sr., was witness to the baptism of Robert, son of Dr. James Skarchinner, "Chirurgeon," on October 22, 1595, and of Violet, daughter of John Jackson, an "Inglishman," in July, 1600.

[9] This name (Smelius) can be rendered in various ways in English or Scots; compare George F. Black, *The Surnames of Scotland, their Origin, Meaning, and History*, New York, 1946, particularly under Smalley and Smellie.

[10] Frank Isaac, *English Printers' Types of the Sixteenth Century*, Oxford, 1936, pp. 48-50.

the continent for sale in Britain, which the Dunkirkers had confiscated.

As to the value of these goods, it is possible to be more exact. Fynes Moryson's *Itinerary* (London, John Beale, 1617, sign. ¶8) informs us that "20 stiuers [make] a gulden or three shillings foure pence, being two shillings English"; consequently the thousand guldens which constituted Waldegrave's loss were equal to two thousand English shillings, one hundred pounds, or two hundred golden angels. In order to arrive at the present-day value of this sum, it is generally customary to multiply the total by some arbitrary figure. This has always seemed to me a most unsatisfactory procedure, especially so for this particular period, since more practical standards for comparison are available. These will make it more apparent than any arbitrary figure can ever do that in 1603 a thousand guldens or a hundred English pounds was a very handsome sum indeed. In 1618 the house rent of a London baker's family was estimated at thirty pounds annually.[11] The chatty Moryson has preserved for us a wealth of detail in regard to the cost of living and travelling expenses in the closing years of the sixteenth century. For more or less permanent expatriates, Moryson estimated (sign. 3E6) that "fifty or sixty pounds sterling yeerely, were sufficient at the time when I was beyond sea, to beare the charge of a Trauellers diet, necessary apparrell, and two iournies yeerely, in the Spring and Autumne." Again, at Leyden in 1592, Moryson says (sign. D5^v) that he paid for his "diet and chamber in this French-mans house three guldens, and fifteene stiuers weekly, but in the common Innes they pay ten or fifteene stiuers a meale, according to the quantity of beere they drinke, and ordinarily twenty stiuers or more, if they drinke wine." Finally he states in his general summary (sign. 3I4): "In the publike Innes a passenger paies some ten or fourteene stiuers each meale: but if he drinke wine, that will cost as much more, by reason of the great impositions vpon the Wines. Besides that, the Flemmings his consorts drinking beare stiffely, especially if they light vpon English beare, and drinke being put into the common reckoning of the company, a stranger shall pay for their intemperancy."

---

[11] *Shakespeare's England, An Account of the Life & Manners of his Age*, Oxford, 1916, I, 318.

The sum of a thousand guldens, then, was the equivalent of a three-years' rent for a London baker; for this amount a traveller could live abroad for nearly two years, or five Englishmen could live "American plan" at Leyden for a period of twelve months; and, finally, with this much money one would have been able to give a banquet complete with wines for a thousand guests in the fair city of Amsterdam. A thousand guldens was, in short, a very considerable sum of money in 1603, and one might conjecture that it had the purchasing power of approximately six to eight thousand dollars of our money.

When one considers that Waldegrave's means two decades earlier were not sufficient to prevent his being thrown into jail at least twice, that he had appeared in Edinburgh as a fugitive just a dozen years before, and that the goods which the Dunkirkers had appropriated could hardly have represented the entire capital of the firm, one can only conclude that Waldegrave had done very well for himself in the Scottish capital. His return to London shortly after the date of this letter must have been a great personal triumph for the former vagrant-printer, and it is safe to assume that he was no longer quite so opposed to the rights of the privileged printers or to the principles of the established church as he once had been.

the pinchpenny bibliophile

By BARROWS MUSSEY

I HAVE always distinguished sharply between a great collector and the author of a great collection. Mr. Morgan and Mr. Lenox could have formed their libraries just as well without being half such smart men as they were: they had only to write a check for any rarity they wanted. When you get down into Mussey's league (about Class E) you have to be a great collector to have any collection at all.

I will now give the rules by which I have formed, at a cost of less than a thousand dollars and in two years' time, the finest collection of rare books anywhere within seven and a half miles (or the distance to our public library).

Rule One: A collector's time is not money, or, What's time to a hog? If you figure your time at even the legal minimum of fifty-five cents an hour, your collection is going to cost you a fortune regardless.

When you have Rule One firmly ingrained in your consciousness, you can start rooting through ten-cent counters, leaky cartons of Laura Jean Libbey at country auctions, and the dark corners in second-hand furniture stores. This is known in bibliophilic circles by the more dignified name of "hunting for sleepers"; but like Chico Marx's price for not rehearsing his band, at hourly rates you couldn't afford it under any name.

Reading book catalogues is a mild form of the same economy. Unless your tastes are very odd indeed (of which more in a moment), there are one or two dealers who specialize in just what you want. They take considerable trouble to bring you and your special wants together, and for this trouble they have to be paid. You, accordingly, will follow Rule One and shun their catalogues except as necessary under Rule Six, *infra*, and will study the smeary mimeographed lists of amateur dealers in out-of-the-way places. These dealers often show a laudable tendency to price books according to literary reputation, date, condition, or some other logical scale, through whose chinks the pinchpenny bibliophile darts ferretlike to snatch something that is not very famous, not very old, or not very well preserved—say a slightly shaken second edition of Chester Harding's autobiography at twenty-five cents. (Actually, that once came from a Fourth Avenue counter.)

The rabid follower of Rule One will not, as a matter of fact, have much truck with catalogues at all. Even the books that cost the dealer nothing originally—and they are many—cost him twenty-five or fifty cents to catalogue, plus wrapping and postage for the book. And the true pinchpenny bibliophile feels generous when he pays a quarter for the privilege of entering a bookseller's premises and spotting a book on the shelves.

For myself I can't follow Rule One all the way out to the end, because my nearest bookseller friends are twenty miles away. My travel time is by definition worth nothing, but there is no pinchpenny method of buying gasoline.

Haste Makes Waste

Rule Two: Don't collect rarities because they're rare. Lay off the Bay Psalm Book unless you are collecting hymnals; and if what you want is hymns, why not a facsimile edition?

The simple basis of rarity prices is awfully easy to forget, so let me remind you. A unique item with no potential buyer (for instance, an autographed letter from me to a bookseller, complaining of his prices) is waste paper, worth nothing even to my good friend Warshaw's Collection of Business Americana. A unique item with one potential buyer—say the death warrant of an ancestor who was executed for piracy—is worth whatever buyer and seller can agree on: in this supposititious instance, maybe a dollar. A unique item with two potential buyers is worth the bottom dollar of the richer aspirant. It will thus be seen that the pinchpenny bibliophile concentrates strongly on the second class of rarity.

This rule is hard to follow, of course, if you *have* spent forty years and two or three hundred dollars assembling every hymnal published in the United States, and then find Parke-Bernet flaunting a *Whole Book of Psalmes* right under your nose. But so long as you want it for a purpose, not for its mere scarcity, Rule Two will not banish you into the ranks of free spenders.

Rule Two is really just another way of stating Rule Three, which is the keystone of my whole structure and the only way to save important money in book-collecting.

Too Many Cooks Spoil the Broth

Rule Three: Be your own expert. Collect for your own purposes, not for A. Edward Newton's.

I read somewhere recently that what book-collecting needs is another Newton to write persuasive gems about it. I disagree flatly.

What book-collecting needs is about twenty thousand John Smiths to make twenty thousand different collections covering, for instance, engravings of the aardvark, or the public documents of East Chicago, Indiana, or the literature of ships in bottles. This would bring together a great many unique items and unique buyers, widen the range of scholarship, and give twenty thousand people a more useful and legitimate collecting satisfaction than that of the one man on whose wallet the auctioneer's hammer falls in knocking down a Lincoln letter for five thousand dollars.

I am forever astonished at the endless fields of interest that people cannot even be bullied into exploring. Take for instance industrial history. True, the old warhorses like C. P. Everitt once priced at fifty cents the Chauncey Jerome's *American Clock Making* that they now get ten dollars for; but how many educated businessmen collect the histories of their own industries?

Book publishers should be more alive than almost any other group to the riches of their own history, so closely entwined with both literature and art. Yet it took me less than ten years and a very few hundred dollars to assemble the best private collection on publishing in the country. That was burned, and I have now devoted the worthless (Rule One) spare time of three months to reassembling possibly a fifth of the old lot, plus some I never had before. And who has offered what feeble competition there is? Publishers? Not on your tintype. Bibliographers, local historians, and the A. Edward Newtons whom I so deplore.

One of my dear friends, an Ivy League Phi Beta Kappa, buys more current books in a month than I do in a year. But until he wanted some pictures to frame for his office he had never even thought of old books on his own textile trade.

Rule Three is more than just a money-saver, it's good for your soul. If you know why you want what you want, you make your own rules and "points." You don't have to invent rationalizations for following Merle Johnson and the fashion. The claims of literary insights to be found in modern first editions always make me feel as Dr. Johnson felt about arguments that proved poverty was beneficial. He said you never found anyone endeavoring to convince you that wealth was a good thing.

I can't for the life of me understand why anyone wants a Hemingway first; but some of the people who do want them undoubtedly have quite as good reasons as I have for wanting the complete output of John Warner Barber.

I collect American views for the simple purpose of reproducing them in picture books. A set of Wall's *Hudson River Portfolio* brought $1700, but I don't envy the fortunate buyer, because nearly all of the twenty views are copied in the crisp little wood engravings sprinkled through the pages of Goodrich's *Pictorial Geography*, which I buy on each of the frequent occasions when I can get a copy for fifty cents. The wood engravings reproduce better than the originals, too. See Rule Six. Having thus become a connoisseur of Goodrich's *Pictorial Geography*, I thought it legitimate recently to pick up a first edition. Nine hundred and twenty-two pages, full contemporary calf, thirty-five cents.

The next rule again is just a variant of Rule Three.

All is Well That Ends Well

Rule Four: Don't collect "condition" unless it means something. Wilmarth S. Lewis very properly keeps trading-up in his Horace Walpole collection, because he wants a perfect copy of everything Walpole ever had anything to do with. But the pinchpenny bibliophile probably wants his books to read, or, in extreme cases, to cut up. If you will put out real cash just to avoid a few sprung signatures or a flapping backstrip, you can't play on our team. Of course when you already have, say, all the known works of Bud Fisher, that's different; you can start swapping off dog-eared copies for clean ones. See Practical Hints.

A model for the pinchpenny collector in this respect is an old friend who writes recipes under a female name. What brings the brightest gleam to *his* eye is an old cookbook with the covers torn off. He is practically willing to pay a bonus for them without covers because they are easier to store and file. Here he very nearly offends against Rule One—he should not count his labor in stripping the books. But after all, with him it is business as well as pleasure.

Rule Five: The tightwad's answer—Know, know, know!

Rival booksellers sometimes suffer attacks of righteous indignation when a competitor has given an old colored woman twenty-five cents for a decrepit suitcase containing a copy of Poe's *Tamerlane*.

While of course I too would rather have this happen to me than to somebody else, speaking generally I think it occurs far too seldom nowadays. Using your knowledge is just a kinder name for profiting by other people's ignorance, and ultimately it is the only way any collector can collect, or any dealer in antiquities make a living. A copy of *Tamerlane* is worth exactly as much as a defective *Poems of Passion* until it falls under the eye of someone who has spent a lifetime learning to tell them apart. His knowledge actually creates the value. Two bits is a very fair return to the colored woman for not throwing away the suitcase given to her by a former employer. And the former employer was well rid of something that her (perfectly legitimate) ignorance made into waste paper.

Note, furthermore, the close interlocking of my rules. By attending to Rule Three you have a foolproof system. No one else can possibly know your weaknesses. What bookseller, however learned, can pounce on an S. G. Goodrich Hartford imprint, turn to his shelf of Blanck, Johnson, and auction records, and then muse ominously, "Hmm, that Mussey will really pay for this"? No reference book will tell him that I collect Goodrich because he was a publisher and a big employer of wood engravers. The Peter Parley volumes that Hawthorne ghosted are worth less to me than the early ones with nicer illustrations. But what reasonable collector would act from such eccentric motives?

Of course the bookseller may rescue a set of Goodrich's *Recollections of a Lifetime* from some ashcan, and sell it to me for three dollars: this I am glad to have him do, for otherwise he could not survive and feed me the J. W. Barbers that my addiction demands.

All in all, though, my system is calculated to foil book-scout and forger alike, bilking them of a proper livelihood, while Rule One absorbs the brunt of my doing their work for them.

KNOWLEDGE IS POWER

Rule Five should be taken in its widest significance—it isn't only what you know, it's whom you know. I frankly advocate trading on other people's good nature as well as on their ignorance.

This means you have likewise to let them trade on yours, and I'm in favor of that, too. I want more successful pinchpenny bibliophiles, not fewer.

The primary purpose of making friends with booksellers is to make friends; but success brings you a double bonus. You find what you want, and you save money on it. In fact, under Rule Five you get a triple bonus, because you can't consort with any self-respecting rare-bookseller and not come away wiser than you went. Charlie Everitt's conversation would certainly be worth a hundred dollars an hour in cash to me if I could just remember it all, and he gives it away free—not even fifteen minutes with each pound of *Latter-Day Saints' Emigrants' Guide.*

On the other hand, if I chanced upon Brigham Young's holograph proposal to wife number seven, I would joyfully pass it on to Charlie at cost. I live in a collecting fool's paradise east of the Ohio, and I think Western rarities should go where they're appreciated. (See Rule Two.)

Rule Five, Corollary One: Don't forget what you were doing. In a collecting contest between a long memory and a long pocketbook, the memory will win every time. If you see a Dover, 1807, edition of Henry Tufts's *Narrative,* and don't remember that Samuel Bragg's printing plant burned soon afterward, you will grudge a dollar, and pay twenty later to someone who does remember. I paid an auctioneer a dollar and a half for reminding me that Lackington's *Memoirs* and *Confessions* are not the same, but I regret almost more the dimes and quarters that trickle out through the leaks in my memory of which

Prove All Things, Hold Fast That Which is Good

Peter Parley and Jacob Abbott titles I already own. I am half tempted to define a great collector as one who can remember what he's got.

Practical Hints on Skinning Flints:

Since by reading this far you have ranked yourself among those who will spend anything sooner than money, I next list a few concrete extensions (or should I say flying buttresses?) of the Mussey System for beating the bookies.

Use your imagination. If you follow Rule Three, your wants will be so obscure that you can seldom fill them without first imagining where you would go if you were, so to speak, a jackass. My Railroad illustrations are Lawrence Romaine's Transportation, Wright Howes's Travel, Benjamin Rosenzweig's West, David Low's Americana, and somebody else's Miscellaneous. And you know what happens to the collector of ships in bottles who looks under Curiosa. He would do much better to try Arts and Crafts, or possibly Marine (sometimes, of course, the cataloguer helps out with two separate headings, first Curiosa and then Curious).

Keep a card index of the ones that got away. You may be a great collector, and hence able to remember everything you have. But it takes more than that, it takes genius, to remember the publisher, date, and collation of everything you *hope* to have.

When some bookseller who does not sympathize with pinchpenny bibliophily catalogues *An Oneida County Printer: William Williams* at fifteen dollars, or an auctioneer casts the vulgar light of competition on a Bewick's *British Quadrupeds,* I paste the item in my hat, or rather in my card index. There'll be another copy along if I can just remember to reach out and take it. (And see under Rule Six.)

Buy in lots. Nothing looks so valuable as a single book. If you will cart away some other trash with it, you can earn a rebate. And here I shall betray perhaps the only trade secret I know, which we will christen (not accurately after its inventor) the Prager Method:

Don't look through the books past the title; don't count them; dump them on the floor, not a table; and simply ask, "How much for that lot?"

The Prager Method is not infallible, because some excessively neat vendors will scrutinize the books, count them, and actually pick them up. But even then your crude insensitivity to the finer values of literature and typography will probably save you a dollar or two. A random heap of books and mouse-dung on the floor looks an awful lot smaller than the same books dusted and ranged on a shelf.

The Prager Method will get you plenty of books you don't want, along with some that you wanted more before you had three other copies. This is one of its most valuable features. Without the discards how could you swap?

I have repeatedly traded my discards, not to other collectors but to hard-bitten booksellers, and come out ahead—*i.e.*, instead of owing twenty-five dollars I would return from a fifty-mile drive owing only twenty-two fifty. Not everyone can be so fortunate, but my example may give you something to shoot at.

Slow but Sure

Rule Six: Count your paper profits. This may not be the most valuable part of my system, but it is the only original one. It has rarity, if not potential takers.

When I have spotted a book on octagonal houses because it shows the nut-shaped mansion of O. S. Fowler, who was a publisher as well as a phrenologist (and my grandfather's first employer); have ascertained that it lacks part of one page and has a hinge gone; have jumbled it on the floor along with a dozen Hale's American Histories and

Mitchell's Geographies; have bought the lot at an average price of 11.54 cents; and have traded off the Hales to reduce an overdue bill; then I am only half done saving money.

I now begin looking for the octagon title in catalogues. If I find it listed at three dollars, I can credit myself with a profit of $2.8946. Probably I shall have the eventual satisfaction of seeing that some specialist in architectural books has catalogued it at $7.50. The savings under Rule Six rapidly become astronomical, if you don't mind where the decimal point is.

The rule has its pitfalls, though, like any pioneer improvement. Years ago I bought for half a dollar a fat and very interesting tome called *Great Industries of the United States*. Afterward, in obedience to Rule Six, I kept marking up savings of from $2.50 to $4.50; it became a regular habit. Then a copy appeared in a country auction with a mess of Dr. Chase's recipe books and similar rough diamonds. I felt at the time that Rule Six made a fifty-cent bid practically mandatory. Soon afterward an industry-minded bookseller raised the *Great Industries* ceiling to six dollars, and consequently I couldn't bear to leave behind the next copy I found for thirty-five cents in an executor's sale.

By now I daren't tell you how many copies of *Great Industries* adorn my shelves, thanks entirely to that confounded Rule Six.

Much Coin, Much Care

JEFFERSON, FRENEAU, And the *Poems* of 1809

By WILLIAM PEDEN

AMONG the four American poets included in the library which Thomas Jefferson spent almost half a century collecting was the "Poet of the American Revolution," Philip Freneau. Freneau had served Jefferson and the Republican cause ably during the stirring days of the Federalist-Republican struggle. As editor of the anti-Hamilton *National Gazette,* he had earned Jefferson's gratitude during the celebrated "War of the Gazettes." Although President George Washington had angrily dubbed him "that rascal, Freneau," Secretary of State Jefferson insisted that Freneau's "paper has saved our constitution" and referred to him as a "man of genius." So it is hardly surprising that in later years Freneau was included, along with Barlow, Dwight, and Trumbull, in the collection which one of Jefferson's contemporaries described as a "library which, for its selection, rarity, and intrinsic value, is beyond all price."

Freneau was represented in this library by two editions, the Monmouth collection of 1795, and the standard edition: *Poems | written and published during the | American Revolutionary War, | and now | republished from the original Manuscripts; | interspersed | with Translations from the Ancients, | and other Pieces not heretofore in | Print. | By Philip Freneau. | . . . | Philadelphia: | From the Press of Lydia R. Bailey, . . . | 1809. |* Concerning this two-volume edition, and Jefferson's subscription to it, some data are available (largely based on manuscript materials in the Library of Congress and elsewhere) which involve not only Jefferson and Freneau but President James Madison and Lydia Bailey, Freneau's publisher.

Early in 1809 Freneau learned that Lydia Bailey was planning to publish a two-volume edition of his collected poems. No kin to Kenneth Roberts's heroine of the same name, Lydia Bailey was an able and aggressive woman, one of Philadelphia's first women printers, and the daughter-in-law of Francis Bailey, who had been Freneau's friend and publisher. Her husband, Robert Bailey, had died in 1808, and Mrs. Bailey's financial condition was, to say the least, precarious. Largely for this reason, Freneau assented to the republication of the "old Scribblings" which at one time he had wished to let "float quietly down the stream of oblivion to their destined element the ocean of forgetfulness." But he was anxious to avoid the errors which had marred earlier editions of his work, and so he went to Philadelphia to supervise the publication which had been started without his knowledge or consent:

I hope you will credit me [he informed his old friend and one-time Princeton classmate James Madison] when I say that the republication of these poems, such as they are, was not a business of my own seeking or forwarding.... However, I have concluded to remain here this Summer, and have them published in a respectable manner, and free as possible from the blemishes imputable to the two former Editions, over which I had no controul, having given my manuscripts away, and left them to the Mercy of chance.

From Philadelphia, on April 8, 1809, Freneau wrote to Jefferson at Monticello concerning the new edition as follows:

I do myself the pleasure to enclose to you a copy of Proposals for the publication of a couple of volumes of Poems shortly to be put to press in this city. Perhaps some of your particular friends in Virginia may be induced from a view of the proposals in your hands to subscribe their names. If so, please to have them forwarded to this place by Post, addressed to the Publisher at No. 10, North Alley, Philadelphia....

On the same day, the ambitious author wrote an almost identical letter to recently-inaugurated President Madison. The response, states Freneau's biographer Lewis Leary, "was immediately satisfactory. Jefferson and Madison each subscribed for ten sets." The response was indeed satisfactory; Mr. Leary records the fact that "1026 copies... were ordered in advance of publication by 403 subscribers," including Madison and Jefferson. Madison, it is true, ordered ten copies of the forthcoming edition. Jefferson also subscribed, but not, as we shall see, for ten sets.

Madison's reply to Freneau's inquiry seems not to have survived. Freneau's answer to Madison, on the other hand, does exist, and shows that the President did subscribe for ten sets. On May 12, 1809, Freneau wrote Madison acknowledging his letter, which he found "on Mrs. Bailey's table." Fifteen hundred copies are to be printed, Freneau continues (expressing the belief that "three times that number might soon be disposed of"), and promises to "forward the *ten* [italics mine] you mention by the middle of July or sooner."

Jefferson, enjoying to the full his long-anticipated retirement, was less prompt than Madison in answering Freneau's letter of April 8th. Not until May 22d did he reply, subscribing "with pleasure" for himself and explaining why he had not seen fit to circulate Freneau's prospectus among his neighbors in Albemarle. It will be noted that nowhere does Jefferson mention any specific number of sets:

> I subscribe with pleasure to the publication of your volumes of poems. I anticipate the same pleasure from them which the perusal of those heretofore published has given me. I have not been able to circulate the paper because I have not been from home above once or twice since my return, and because in a country situation like mine, little can be done in that way. the inhabitants of the country are mostly industrious farmers employed in active life & reading little. they rarely buy a book of whose merit they can not judge by having it in their hand, & are less disposed to engage for those yet unknown to them. I am becoming like them myself in a preference of the healthy & chearful environment without doors, to the being immured within four brick walls. but under the shade of a tree one of your volumes will be a pleasant pocket companion. wishing you all possible success & happiness, I salute you with constant esteem & respect.

Five days later, on May 27th, Freneau replied, assuring Jefferson that he had "only wished your name to be placed at the head of the [subscription] list, and did not wish you to be at the pains of collecting subscriptions." He states that he will be happy if his "two little Volumes" amuse Jefferson "but for a single hour," and concludes:

> This is the first edition that I have in reality attended to, the other two having been published, in a strange way, from manuscripts left to the drifting of the winds, while I was wandering over gloomy seas, until *embargoed* [italics Freneau's] by the necessity of the times, and now again, I fear, I am reverting to the folly of scribbling verses.

In August, approximately three months later, the volumes were through the press. On August 7th Freneau was able to write Madison from Philadelphia that

> The two Volumes of Poems that in April last I engaged to have published, are finished, and will be ready for delivery in two or three days. The ten setts you subscribed for I am rather at a loss how to have safely transmitted to you.... [Madison was not in Washington at this time, and Freneau had heard that he intended to remain in Virginia until the end of September.]

The *Poems* of 1809 appeared in two bindings—sheep, retailing at two dollars a set, and calf, at two dollars and twenty-five cents. With their publication, Freneau's responsibility ended. But Mrs. Bailey's continued. That she did not always discharge this responsibility as efficiently as might have been desired is evident from subsequent correspondence. The books were not forwarded to Jefferson at Monticello until several months after publication, and then were relayed to him by Madison, who frequently aided Jefferson in his book-buying, just as Jefferson had for so many years aided Madison in his. It is difficult to understand the reasons for Mrs. Bailey's delay. However busy she may have been, it is extremely strange that Jefferson's subscription, whether it was for one or for one hundred sets, did not receive her immediate attention. At any rate, not until March 22, 1810, did she inform him that she was billing him for ten sets at two dollars a set:

> By this days mail stage [she wrote], I forward to you a box containing eleven Copies Freneaus Poems directed to the care of James Madison President. you will please accept the copy bound in calf. also the pocket Almanac. I thank you for your very liberal Subscription to the Poems.

Jefferson answered with some consternation on April 18th, acknowledging Mrs. Bailey's letter, expressing his respect for and admiration of Freneau, but insisting that there must have been some mistake, as he never, under any circumstances, subscribed for more than two copies of "any work":

> I have recieved the favor of your letter of Mar. 22. in which I think there must be some mistake in ascribing to me a subscription for *ten* [italics Jefferson's] copies of mr Freneau's poems. certainly if I ever had subscribed for that number from any

one, from principles of great esteem, it was as likely to be him as any one, for whom I have a very high esteem, of which I hope he can never entertain a doubt. but as I never did, to my recollection subscribe for more than two copies of any work, I conclude there must be an error in this instance. I must pray you therefore to re-examine your subscription papers and if you find I have annexed that number to my subscription, be so good as to favor me with another line of information & I shall fulfill the engagement. in the mean time accept the assurances of my respect.

Mrs. Bailey seems to have received this letter with a degree of surprise comparable to Jefferson's, but she replied on May 8, 1810, with equal courtesy:

I have received the favour of your letter of April 18 in which [sic] I regret the mistake relative to your Subscription to Freneaus Poems I have examined agreeable to your request the Subscription papers and find your name for 10 Copies, but when compared with your letter the hand does not by any means corespond with that of yours Some person wanting principle must have taken the unwarentable liberty and what object they could have in view I know not—If you think proper you will please returne the Poems to me in the mean time accept the assurance of my highest respect.

Jefferson did not reply until nearly seven months later. His letter, dated December 6, 1810, fails to throw any light on the identity of the "person wanting principle" whom Mrs. Bailey suspected of causing the misunderstanding:

The 10. copies of Freneau's poems which were forwarded to me thro the President of the US. were a considerable time getting to me and owing to my other occupations they have remained longer unattended to than ought to have been. your letter of May 8. desired me to return them to you. as this must be thro' Richmond, where there would be a probability of disposing of them, I have forwarded the box to mr Pritchard bookseller there, formerly of Philadelphia & probably known to you, with a request that he would hold them subject to your order, either for sale there, or to be forwarded to you in Philadelphia, & in the mean time not to omit any opportunity of selling them for your benefit. you will be so good therefore as to give him your instructions on this subject. the two copies I subscribed for shall be paid thro' him, it being difficult to remit small fractional sums from this place to Philadelphia. accept the assurances of my respect.

On the same day, Jefferson explained the situation to the Richmond bookseller. William Pri(t)chard, a Philadelphia auctioneer and book dealer, had sold books to Jefferson since the early 1780's. After moving to Richmond, he acted as Jefferson's agent in that city.

A circumstance which will be explained [Jefferson wrote from Monticello on December 6] induces me to recall to your recollection an old acquaintance and customer while you lived in Philadelphia. I subscribed to mrs Lydia R. Bailey of Philadelphia for 2. copies of Freneau's poems which she was about to print. by some mistake, 10. copies were sent. they were addressed thro' the President of the US. whose business probably prevented their being immediately forwarded, and mine has for some time prevented my attending to them. on apprising mrs Bailey of the mistake she desired I would return them to Philadelphia. desirous of having them sold for her if I can, I have thought it better to forward them to you with a request that you will hold either them or their proceeds, if you can sell them, . . . these . . . are now forwarded by a boat. . . . Accept my friendly salutations & assurances of esteem & respect

With this letter to Pritchard, who presumably carried out Jefferson's instructions, the matter—as far as factual evidence is concerned—ends. One or two questions, however, remain.

Concerning the initial misunderstanding of Jefferson's supposed subscription to ten sets of the *Poems* of 1809—a subscription which we have seen that Jefferson never made—it appears quite impossible to consider seriously Mrs. Bailey's rather naïve assumption that some scoundrel forged Jefferson's name on the subscription papers. Nor is it at all likely that Mrs. Bailey deliberately attempted to hoodwink Jefferson into purchasing more copies than he had subscribed for. It is quite possible, however, that she hoped and believed that Jefferson might pay for the extra copies rather than go to the trouble of returning them. It is equally difficult to accuse Freneau of being the source of the confusion. On the other hand, he might have assumed that Jefferson would subscribe for as many sets as had Madison. It is conceivable that he might have entered, or directed an employee of Mrs. Bailey to enter, such an order in Mrs. Bailey's waste-book or record of accounts.[1]

[1] Mrs. Bailey's record, fragmentary and incomplete as it is, fails to answer the question. Lewis Leary, Freneau's biographer, informs me that on pp. 18-21 of Mrs. Bailey's waste-book there is a list "of the subscribers for Freneaus Poems to home they have been delivered as follows" (totalling 235 copies), but neither Jefferson nor Madison is mentioned. Both Madison and Jefferson are listed, however, in the printed list of subscribers included in the 1809 edition, and each is listed as having subscribed for ten copies.

Jefferson's unreturned set of the *Poems* was included in his personal library of some 6,500 volumes which he sold to Congress in January, 1815, after the original Library of Congress had been destroyed by the British, but it is no longer extant; apparently it was among the casualties of the disastrous fire of 1851 which consumed approximately two-thirds of the Jefferson collection along with all but some 20,000 of the 55,000 volumes constituting the Library at that time. Madison's library, unfortunately, was scattered to the four winds after his death, and the fate of his copies of Freneau is not known.

At any rate, Jefferson was now through with subscription buying in general, although it would be unjust and inaccurate to lay the cause at Mrs. Bailey's door alone. Among the manuscript letters Jefferson wrote during his retirement, there are occasional references to subscription buying (for example, in 1813, he subscribed to James Cutbush's *American Artists Manual,* and to John Garnett's *Nautical Almanac* in 1815). But these were rare exceptions. And when Samuel Whitcomb, of Dorchester, Massachusetts, attempted to enlist Jefferson's interest in an unpublished book, he was abruptly refused. In recording his interview with Jefferson in 1824 Whitcomb relates: "Between 8 & 9 o'clk called on Mr. Jefferson. The boy conducted and left me at the door and I knocked. Mr. Jefferson came himself. I approached and shook hands with him and he asked me in. I opened by saying I had no introduction to him but a new publication for which I was getting subscribers. He replied he never subscribed for anything."

NOTE: I wish to express my thanks to those who have aided me with specific information and suggestions: Prof. Lewis Leary, Freneau's biographer; Miss E. M. Sowerby, bibliographer of the Jefferson Library, Library of Congress; and Mr. Julian Boyd, librarian of Princeton University. I wish also to thank Mr. Stewart Mitchell, Director of the Massachusetts Historical Society, for permission to reprint Jefferson's letter to Pritchard of Dec. 6, 1810, as well as the excerpt from Samuel Whitcomb's interview with Jefferson, May 31, 1824. I wish finally to thank Mr. Frederick W. Wead of Boston and the staffs of the Library of Congress and the University of Virginia for their assistance.—W. P.

The Court of Appeals

To adjust the minute events of literary history is tedious and troublesome; it requires indeed no great force of understanding, but often depends upon enquiries which there is no opportunity of making, or is to be fetched from books and pamphlets not always at hand.
    John Dryden—LIVES OF THE POETS.

Descriptive bibliography is not in itself a very important study. It is important only as it is ancillary to historical and literary criticism. But it is not for the bibliographer to decide what is of value to his betters; his business is to record the facts.   R. W. Chapman—CANCELS.

APPEAL 20

BRET HARTE IN SUNLIGHT

CAN you tell me anything of a little booklet in my possession containing a Bret Harte poem? It is 32 pages, 4$\frac{13}{16}$ x 6⅛ inches, brown illustrated paper wrappers. The front cover reads: L. B. Ld. SUNLIGHT, by George Augustus Sala, Bret Harte, Joseph Hatton and Geo. R. Sims. Illustrated by Enoch Ward, L. Raven Hill, W. H. Margetson.

The Harte contribution is "The Home-Coming of Jim Wilkes." The only hint of date is that 17 Exposition awards to Sunlight Soap are listed, the latest being 1892. Is this the first appearance of this Harte item and, if so, when was it issued?

PAUL W. KIESER

APPEAL 21

ROCK ME TO SLEEP

MERLE Johnson in *You Know These Lines* states that "the earliest known book appearance of Elizabeth Akers' 'Rock me to sleep' with its well-known lines 'Backward, turn backward, O Time in your flight,' is in *Gathered Waifs*, New Haven: 1864." I have *The Lady's Almanac for the Year 1862*, which publishes the poem anonymously (p. 61-62). Is this, then, the actual first printing in book-form? And has the authorship of this poem ever been definitely established?

EDWARD NAUMBURG, JR.

APPEAL 22

DOYLE'S A STUDY IN SCARLET

I KNOW that Doyle's *A Study in Scarlet* (London: Ward, Lock & Co., 1888), the first appearance in book-form of Sherlock Holmes, is an uncommon book. The only copies appearing at auction in America (1936 and 1944, Parke-Bernet Galleries) were catalogued as: "First issue, with the word *younger* misspelled *youuger* in the second paragraph, third line, of the publisher's preface. This was later corrected." I have heard elsewhere that this "point" is not accurate.

Is there any evidence on this point other than the Parke-Bernet's dictum?

J. S. ECCLES

APPEAL 23

VARIANT BINDINGS ON STEINBECK FIRSTS

I HAVE noticed several John Steinbeck firsts (especially *A Russian Journal*) occurring in

401

variant bindings. Is there any provable priority between these and if so where can the information be obtained?

JOHN S. VAN E. KOHN

APPEAL 24

RARITY OF GREAT EXPECTATIONS

Is there any sound explanation for the rarity of the first edition of Dickens's *Great Expectations*, 1861, in its original three-decker form? Generally, the later books of a well-known author are relatively more common than his earlier ones, as more were printed, but this is not the case here.

PHILO CALHOUN

Findings of the Court

Unsigned answers or comments are by the referee of this department

ANSWER TO APPEAL 19

THE most recent bibliography of Crane, by Ames Williams and Vincent Starrett, states: "No copy of the Philadelphia edition (of *Last Words*) alleged to have been published by Henry T. Coates and Company has been discovered. The records of the company reveal no entry pertaining to such a title and it is probable that the edition is apocryphal."

Now it may be true that the company has no records of this book (the records of most publishing houses are notoriously imperfect), yet the fact remains that Coates did list it on at least two occasions—in the "Spring Announcements" issue of *The Publisher's Weekly*, March 15, 1902, and again in the "Fall Announcements" issue of September 27, 1902.

It was just about this time that they were taken over by John Winston of Philadelphia, and the *U. S. Catalogue Supplement of Books Published 1902-05* lists:

Last Words (Griffin ser). D. il. $1. '02 Winston—with the note "(partially protected fiction)."

Now whether Winston ever issued the book we do not know. Certainly no copy has ever been seen by us. But the evidence for the possibility of its existence is stronger than the Williams-Starrett statement allows.

As to the variant copyrights on *Whilomville Stories* (New York and London, 1900), one in the name of Stephen Crane, the other in the name of his brother, William Howe Crane, it seems logical that the former is the earlier; certainly it is the rarer, and of this variant only the copyright copy in the library of Congress has been found to date. It is a posthumous work and probably the copyright was changed, after Crane's death, from his name to his brother's, for legal reasons.

ANSWER TO APPEAL 20

THE pamphlet in question was issued as an advertisement by Lever Brothers, soap manufacturers, hence the L. B. Ld. on the cover: Lever Brothers, Limited.

Lever Brothers stated in a letter to P. K. Foley, now in the American Antiquarian Society, that the pamphlet was issued some time in 1894.

The story appears in *A Protégée of Jack Hamlin's and Other Stories,* Boston: 1894, deposited for copyright January 18, 1894, and published (according to *The Publisher's Weekly*) January 24, 1894. It appeared in England in *The Bell-Ringer of Angel's* in late October, 1894.

It seems highly unlikely that the Lever Brothers' advertising pamphlet could have appeared earlier than the American edition, but further evidence of its actual publication is not obtainable.

JACOB BLANCK

Answer to Appeal 21

THE volume discovered by Mr. Naumburg, *The Lady's Almanac for the Year 1862*, may not be the earliest book appearance of "Rock me to sleep," but it is certainly the earliest so far discovered and outranks the Merle Johnson candidate by a clear three years.

The poem's first known appearance is in *The Saturday Evening Post*, June 9, 1860, and it was set to music and published in Boston the same year.

As to its authorship, it is our opinion that no conclusive evidence has yet been presented either way. Though Burton Stevenson (*Famous Single Poems*), John T. Winterich (*The Colophon*, part 15, 1933), and Merle Johnson have upheld Mrs. Akers' claim to authorship, as astute a student of the problem as Carroll A. Wilson remained unconvinced. He always claimed (along with Bryant) that there was something more than air to Alexander M. W. Ball's claim to authorship.

Answer to Appeal 22

THE statement by the Parke-Bernet Galleries that the first issue of *A Study in Scarlet* has "the word *younger* misspelled *youuger* in the second paragraph, third line, of the publisher's preface" is the exact opposite of the fact. It is a blithe assumption (too common in bibliography) that since a word is misspelled in one copy and correctly spelled in another, it must first have been set incorrectly and later corrected. As Sherlock was the first to say: "The quick inference, the subtle trap" is fatal. And, again, "There is nothing so deceptive as an obvious fact."

Actually the word was originally spelled correctly. At some point in the printing the first signature was completely reset and it was then that the error occurred. The wrappers, advertising and type degeneration, among other things, clearly prove the priority of the correct *younger* issue [A] over the *youuger* [B].

Briefly: the [A] wrappers lack the two lines later added to [B]: "This design, with the exception of the Lettering, is composed with the 'Patent Kalido Mosaic Type.'"

[A] copies have six pages of inserted advertisements at the end and that of "The Select Library of Fiction" is continued on the inside of the back wrapper, ending with item No. 793. The [B] copies have seven pages of inserted advertisements at the end, "The Select Library of Fiction" ending with item No. 884, and the inside back wrapper has a paying advertisement: "Whelpton's Vegetable Purifying Pills." Type degeneration, painfully obvious when the two variants are examined side by side, is equally conclusive. In point of fact, the two may, upon further research, constitute distinct editions, instead of issues, but the order of priority cannot be reversed.

Answer to Appeal 23

ONE is tempted to use the case of the binding variants on recent first editions of John Steinbeck as an excuse for discoursing at length on the fatuity of trying to assemble all such variants, where no priority can be established for any one. The memory is yet green of those adoring followers of Edna St. Vincent Millay who set out to assemble all six different colors of paper wrapper in which Frank Shay, with the idea of attracting attention to the display in the window of his bookshop, chose to bind his 1920 edition of *A Few Figs from Thistles*.

But collectors are fortunately incorrigible, and no amount of philosophy poured on their enthusiasm can extinguish it. These are the facts: let each man set his own course hereafter.

Cannery Row, Viking, 1945, appeared in two colors of cloth, light buff and canary yellow. The first edition was bound in the closing weeks of 1944, when binding materials were scarce. The edition was large, there was not enough light buff cloth available, so the yellow was selected to finish the run. There is no priority of issuance.

The Wayward Bus, Viking, 1947, was issued in a first edition of 100,000 copies, and again, because materials were still scarce, two different types of cloth were used, though this time their colors are so similar that they can only be distinguished by direct comparison. The simplest differentiation is that in one case the blind-stamping of the bus on the front cover shows up as lighter than the rest of the binding, while in the other it shows up as darker. Again, no priority of issuance.

Differences in the binding of *The Pearl*, Viking, 1947, occur only as between editions; there are no variants within the first edition.

A Russian Journal, Viking, 1948, was issued in no less than four variant bindings. The boom time for trade book publishing had gone by, and it now seemed wise to cut down inventory of manufacturing materials by using up odd lots of cloth where this could be done without sacrificing art to mammon. In all four binding states Viking used a combination of cloth back and paper sides, as follows:

A. Sand gray back (Kennett cloth with rough natural finish), dusk blue paper sides (imitative of buckram). Very rare.

B. Sand gray back (Devron cloth with smooth filled finish), same dusk blue paper sides as A. Medium rare.

C. Cream back (Arrestox cloth), same dusk blue paper sides as A and B. Fairly common.

D. Same cream back as C, with peacock blue paper sides (same style of imitation buckram). Most common.

There is no priority of issuance among these four states, but their relative rarity has been indicated.

The foregoing information has been patiently supplied, not without some misgivings as to the sanity of collectors, by my friends Milton Glick and Morris Colman of The Viking Press Inc.

FREDERICK B. ADAMS, JR.

Percy's Reliques
AND ITS CANCEL LEAVES

Percy's *Reliques of Ancient English Poetry* (3 volumes, London: J. Dodsley, 1765) is bibliographically an extremely complicated book.

The first extended account of it was given by L. F. Powell in *The Library*, Fourth Series, Vol. IX, No. 2, September, 1928. The volumes abound in cancels and these are, as he points out, the most interesting part of his examination. In a number of instances, however, he was unable to describe the text of the original uncancelled leaves.

Allen T. Hazen, in his *Samuel Johnson's*

Prefaces & Dedications (New Haven: 1937), corrects several of Mr. Powell's errors but again fails to discover the reasons for several cancels.

Through the courtesy of Harold Greenhill, of Chicago, we have been allowed to examine his unique copy containing a number of the leaves in both states, hence these notes supplementary to the Powell-Hazen findings.

Volume I. Powell lists the following leaves as cancels: A_8, C_2, C_7, G_4, G_5, but says that he never discovered the original text of any of them. Hazen correctly points out that A_8 is not a cancel and that the stub which appears in some copies between A_7 and A_8 is in reality the turn-over of the frontispiece.

Powell says of leaves C_2 and C_7: "I cannot say why Percy made these cancels." In leaf C_2, recto, the changes are in the footnotes. The third footnote, in the original reads (referring to the "Earl Douglas himself being slain on the spot"): "Not by Henry Percy as is represented in this ballad, and by our common historians, as Stow, Speed, &c." In the cancel this reads: "By Henry L. Percy according to this ballad, and our old English historians, as Stow, Speed, &c."

The fourth footnote, in the original reads: "Hotspur (after a long conflict hand to hand) was taken prisoner." In the cancel this reads: "Henry Lord Percy (after a very sharp conflict)" . . . etc.

On the verso of C_2, line 12 reads in the original: (Froissart) "gives the victory decisively to the Scots." The cancel omits the word "decisively." In the original the footnote explaining the word "hoo" says: "Perhaps 'hoolding.'" In the cancel the note is expanded to: "So in Langham's letter concerning Q. Elizabeth's entertainment at Killingworthy Castle, 1575. 12°. p. 61. 'Heer was no ho in devout drinkying.'"

Leaf C_7, verso. Original has spelling, lines 193 and 197: "uppon"—cancel "upon." The cancel adds the following to the footnote:

"For the names in this page and in page 14, see the *Additions,* Ec. at the end of Vol. 3."

Leaves G_4, G_5. Powell states: "I do not know why the cancels were made. It is to be noted, however, that Percy apologizes for inserting the extract from Stephen Hawes's *Palace of Pleasure,* which takes up most of the space; perhaps this extract was substituted for another ballad at the last moment." This surmise is perfectly correct. In the Greenhill copy the ballad printed here is *The Jolly Beggar.* The first appearance of this famous ballad has hitherto been credited to Herd's *The Ancient and Modern Scots Songs,* 1769, p. 46. The authorship of this poem is attributed by tradition to James V of Scotland, as is also that of the ballad *The Gaberlunyie-Man* with which Horace Walpole confuses it in his *Catalogue of Royal and Noble Authors* (II, 202 f., second edition, 1759). The cancel leaves replace *The Jolly Beggar* with Hawes's *The Tower of Doctrine.*

The verso of leaf G_5 begins the ballad *The Child of Elle.* In the original leaf the note to this reads: "—is given from a fragment in the editor's folio Ms: which was (if possible) still more defective and mutilated than *The Marriage of Sir Gawaine,* in the First Volume. The few stanzas, which had the good fortune to escape this fatal wreck, appeared so extremely beautiful, that they excited a strong desire to attempt a completion of the story. The reader will easily discover the supplemental stanzas by their inferiority, and at the same time be inclined to pardon it, when he considers how difficult it must be to imitate the affecting simplicity and artless graces of the original. CHILD was a title sometimes given to a Knight. See above, page 40."

In the replaced leaf this reads: "—is given from a fragment in the editor's folio Ms: which tho' extremely defective and mutilated, appeared to have so much merit, that it excited a strong desire to attempt a completion of the story. The Reader will easily discover the supplemental stanzas by their inferiority and, at the same time, be inclined to pardon it, when he considers how difficult it must be to imitate the affecting simplicity and artless beauties of the original. CHILD was a title sometimes given to a knight. See Gloss."

Volume II. Powell lists the following leaves as cancels: N_7, U_2, U_3, U_4, X_4. Hazen adds U_5, U_6, U_7, pointing out that all the inner leaves of Sig. U were removed, and six leaves of a new sheet were substituted. There is no reason to question this conclusion.

Volume III. Powell lists, and explains the reasons for, the following cancels: B_1, B_3, G_3, G_4, G_5, G_6, H_4, P_3, T_6, T_7, Y_2.

Now Volume III collates irregularly: A (half sheet); b^8; c^4; B-P [2dP.] Q-X^8; Y^5; Z^8. In all known copies, save Greenhill's, three stubs are visible between [Y_5] and Z. Powell remarks merely: "Y_{6-8} were cut away and a new sheet Z substituted." Hazen remarks, rather airily: "Y_6-Y_8 were cut away but since this must have been done before Sheet Z had been printed (or at least it had been determined that they were to be removed), and Z continues without a break from Y_5 verso, I have not considered them to be cancels."

As this is a technical problem in which Drs. Greg and McKerrow disagree (Dr. Hazen siding with McKerrow) it is with some trepidation that we call Dr. Hazen's conclusions airy. Sound as his theory may be, when applied in like circumstance to treatment of any signature *other than the last,* the fact remains that some explanation for leaves Y_{6-8} is needed. And they are cancels.

In the Greenhill copy leaves Y_6 and Y_7 are slit for cancellation, but not removed. Y_6 recto has the *Glossary* from *Tush* to *Yodo:* verso from *Y-built* to *Zouth* (14 entries in double column). Beneath is a nine line note on the letter Z, beginning: "The printers have usually substituted the letter Z. . ." Beneath this note is a printer's ornament. Leaf Y_7 contains: "Additional Notes to Book the First" with the final line: "The End of Volume The First."

The final leaf, Y_8, was utilized to print a cancel for P_3, and this cancel was itself superseded by a second cancel. The original P_3 is still untraced, but copies exist of both cancels. The first contains no cut of St. George; the second contains the cut. The reason for the second cancel, as Powell points out, was that originally Percy had written: "The incidents in this and Ballad 2d are. . ." and in the first edition there being two "2d Ballads," he was forced to substitute "the other ballad of St. George and the Dragon."

Now when Percy decided to make the very confusing interchange of Volume III and Volume I (the note *To the Binder* reads, in part: "the sheets marked Vol I are to be bound up as Volume the Third: and those noted as Volume III as Volume the First") a number of terminal leaves had to be changed. Hence these cancels Y_6 and Y_7.

As eventually published, the text of the *Glossary Tush* to *Zouth* (Y_6 recto and 14 items on verso) was condensed to leaf Z recto. The note beginning: "The printers have usually subsituted the letter Z. . . ," was transferred to the foot of leaf Z_4 (Volume

I). And the contents of leaf [Y$_7$] are enlarged and transferred to leaves [Z$_{6-7}$] to come in the proper sequence in the additions to this third volume.

Reports on additional copies of this book containing any of the original uncancelled leaves would be welcome, as its unusual history is probably not yet fully known.

KIPLING AND THE FREE-MASON LIONS

DeLancey Ferguson has sent along the following collateral notes to his article in the present issue, so in case any readers may decide to search for young Kipling's "tale about a lion-hunter in South Africa who fell among lions who were all Freemasons," here is a list of juvenile periodicals which do *not* contain it:

Good Words for the Young. London: 1869-1871. 3 volumes, continued as *Good Things for the Young of All Ages,* the volume for 1873 only of this continuation having been examined.

The Boys of England. A Young Gentleman's Magazine of Sport, Sensation, Fun and Instruction. London: 1866 ff. "I have examined Volumes 1-3. The contents are dime novels and 'tushery.' It doesn't seem a likely place to seek further for any story so far-fetched as the one about the lions."

Routledge's Every Boy's Annual for 1873. No results; contents distinctly pedestrian.

Chatterbox for 1874. Ditto.

Aunt Judy's Magazine. London: 1866 ff. "I have not yet examined the complete file; so far as I have gone I would not expect to meet any lion-hunters."

"And incidentally," continues Mr. Ferguson, "why doesn't somebody get busy and do a thorough catalogue and bibliography of juvenile fiction of the Victorian era? Until we know much more about what the late Victorians and the Edwardians read in their youth, we can't fully understand how they got the way they were."

David A. Randall

Marginalia

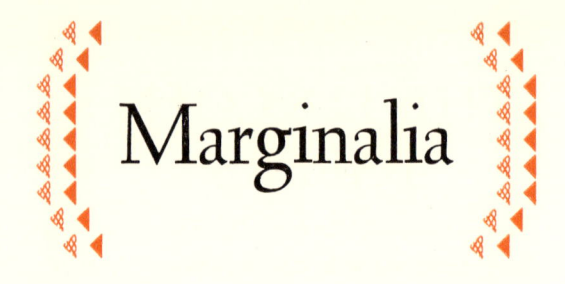

Paul McPharlin—1903-1948

The death of Paul McPharlin on September 28 has not only brought to a premature close the "Scrapbook of Strays" which he wrote for our subscribers but has also deprived those groups concerned with puppetry, printing, and design of one of their most enthusiastic and versatile members. His friendly smile and diverting conversation will be missed at every gathering of his kindred spirits.

Though he was keenly interested in every phase of bookmaking—writing, designing, illustrating, printing, publishing, and collecting—his chief interest undeniably was in puppetry. He helped to found the Puppeteers of America, served as its publications editor, and published several dozen books and pamphlets on the subject. (See *The Annual of Bookmaking*, The Colophon, New York, 1938.) He also directed a professional puppet company for ten years, producing Shakespeare, Fielding, and "minor playwrights, including McPharlin." During a visit to Europe in the spring of 1938 he managed to see ninety puppet shows in ninety days.

Among his achievements as an industrial designer were a conference room, reception area, and offices for the publishing firm of Henry Holt & Company; a chain of candy stores in Chicago; and furniture and fabrics in Detroit. A photograph and his description of the book room he designed for himself are contained in Vol. II, No. 3 of *The Colophon,* New Series, Summer 1937.

In the world of books, Paul McPharlin was extremely active. As a publisher, he issued several classics under the imprint of the Fine Book Circle, and founded its *Fine Book Letter.* As a designer, he did many trade books for Hastings House, Scribner's, and Random House, and for the Limited Editions Club he designed the seven-volume Gibbon *Decline and Fall of the Roman Empire,* with reproductions of the Piranesi etchings. For Didier, he designed and translated from the French Octave Feuillet's *Punch: His Life and Adventures;* and for the Peter Pauper Press he decorated a number of items, including the *Meditations of Marcus Aurelius,* the *Discourses of Epictetus,* and Voltaire's *Satirical Dictionary,* which he also translated. The one book which probably best reflected his bookmaking versatility was *Books In Specimen Pages,* which he designed, compiled and wrote for the North River Press of New York, and which was published in 1947.

The McPharlin by-line has become increasingly familiar in recent years. For *The Publishers' Weekly* he had written thirty bookmaking articles since 1942, including a notable series on great historic books, and another on fine presses and printers. For *The Dolphin,* he edited the "Byways of Bookmaking" department under the pseudonym of Dr. Culrarity. He was a member of the periodical committee of the American Institute of Graphic Arts, contributing to its *Journal* and counselling its publishing program. Two of his books have been published by Hastings House: *Life and Fashion in America, 1650-1900,* and *Love and Courtship in America; Paper Sculpture, Its Construction and Uses* was written for Mar-

ADVERTISEMENTS

The New York Times on August 15, 1948, had this to say about:

Story Classics

"As for most book clubs, members do save money—but do they save the book? *Story Classics* is a kind of book club that escapes the apparent evils of the clubs, perhaps because it is publishing books for discriminating readers, doing those rarely come-by volumes that are a delight to the reading palate, as well as to the eye. *Story Classics'* plan is to bring out these exceptional volumes (illustrated and excellently made) at the rate of six a year, at $3.75 a volume for members."

The first year's titles:
SELECTED SHORT STORIES OF THOMAS HARDY
WHIMSICAL TALES OF DOUGLAS JERROLD
THE CONTINENTAL TALES OF HENRY WADSWORTH LONGFELLOW
TALES FROM THE SPANISH OF ALARCÓN
TALES OF LOVE AND DEATH BY PROSPER MÉRIMÉE
THE BEGGAR AND OTHER STORIES BY ANTON CHEKHOV

Of those issued to date, three have been Monthly Selections of the Trade Book Clinic, A.I.G.A.

For handsome brochure describing the *Story Classics*, write to N. Coe,

STORY CLASSICS
EMMAUS, PENNSYLVANIA

THE LINCOLN PAPERS

Edited by David C. Mearns
Introduction by Carl Sandburg

❧ "The richest, most absorbing lot of historical raw material that has been put in print in a generation."—PAUL ANGLE, author of *The Lincoln Reader*.

❧ The publication of the story of the collection, with selections to July 4, 1861, is the year's outstanding event for Lincoln collectors. The edition is beautifully printed and bound, illustrated and ornamented, in two volumes, boxed. $10.00

DOUBLEDAY & CO., INC.
Garden City, N. Y.

THE Renaissance Painter's Garden

By RUTH WEDGWOOD KENNEDY

With its text completely handset in a famous Bruce Rogers type, its title page hand-painted in 24 colors and gold, and its 60 collotype reproductions of details from the works of Leonardo, Titian, Botticelli and other Italian masters, *The Renaissance Painter's Garden* is a volume that every lover of fine books will want to own.

Limited edition, numbered, $30.00

At all bookstores, or from

OXFORD UNIVERSITY PRESS
114 FIFTH AVENUE, NEW YORK 11

quardt & Company; for the Typophiles, an organization in which he participated actively, he prepared the delightful Chapbook on *Roman Numerals, Typographic Leaves and Pointing Hands* in 1942; Harper's Fall list includes a posthumous publication, *The Puppet Theatre in America; A History.*

A Note on Rudolph Ruzicka

To some readers, the work of the designer may be a complete waste of time. Their eyes and interest are solely on what the author has written, not on how it looks. It would be futile to try to dissuade them, or disturb their convictions.

To others, and their ranks are happily multiplying, what is worth printing is worth printing well—worth making attractive and allusive, worthy of the permanence of print. Few Colophonians need persuasion in this direction.

Evaluating the work of the designer and his contribution can best be done after thoroughly reading the issue. And that is recommended whether you know much of publishing and printing procedure, or little.

In practice, the designer of a periodical like ours receives from the editors the various manuscripts which are to comprise the issue, together with an indication of preference for sequence of position, and the illustrative material essential to each article.

The designer's job is to co-ordinate this material typographically—essentially a matter of fitting words to space and dressing each article attractively. This involves a degree of mathematics for space computation; selection of type faces for body matter and headings; consideration of the need for initials, if any; and decisions about point sizes of type and leading for main and subordinate matter, as well as for departmental texts.

Basically, the work involves a series of compromises between what one would like to do and what can be done with consideration of time, budgets, and physical limitations of material or equipment.

When the designer does his job well, nothing seems forced or contrived, the reader isn't annoyed or distracted by spectacular effects that impinge upon the reading process—there is no interference between author and reader. Nor are the articles displayed in a commonplace, mediocre manner. Instead, the material gains the distinction of presentation that comes from the considered esthetic judgment of a trained and competent artist.

The present issue is the work of Rudolph Ruzicka, one of the more distinguished of American designers, a recipient of the Medal of the American Institute of Graphic Arts, a cultivated man, a fine critic, and a many-sided artist who does a number of totally different things extremely well.

Best known, perhaps, as an engraver on wood and metal, he is in addition uncommonly gifted in designing books and printed pieces. He has completed the design of two type faces for Linotype, of which the first, Fairfield, has been used for setting the text of this issue.

He is a colorist of prime ability too, having been selected by International Printing Ink Corporation to develop and design their authoritative *Three Monographs on Color,* published in 1935.

A few months ago, from mid-April to mid-June, 1948, The Grolier Club (of which Ruzicka is an Honorary Member) held its comprehensive exhibition of his engraved and typographic work. On display were well over two hundred items—representative selections of more than forty years' work—in-

ADVERTISEMENTS

A new and exciting chapter in the Lincoln story

LINCOLN AND THE WAR GOVERNORS

by William B. Hesseltine

PROFESSOR OF HISTORY, UNIVERSITY OF WISCONSIN

The little-known but dramatic story of Lincoln's manipulation of political opinion in the North, of Lincoln locked in conflict with the Northern governors over troops and supplies, of Lincoln transforming a loose federation of sovereign states into a unified and consolidated nation. 437 pages. $4.50

"The approach is new; the research is well presented; the temper is critical but never biased. With rare skill the author has shown again that the Lincoln story is far from being completely told."
—*New York Herald Tribune Book Review*

The first life of William Herndon, Lincoln's friend, law partner, and biographer

LINCOLN'S HERNDON

by David Donald

WITH AN INTRODUCTION BY CARL SANDBURG

This biography is a stirring human document with a two-fold focus: on Lincoln's Illinois days of courting, arguing, and politicking; and on Herndon's own life as Lincoln's law partner, mayor of Springfield, political boss, poet, dreamer, and author of what is probably the most controversial biography ever written, *Herndon's Life of Lincoln*. A great and profoundly moving story that achieves the impetus and grandeur of tragedy. 400 pages. Illustrated. $5.00

Wherever books are sold

Published by ALFRED A. KNOPF, New York 22,
who will send you his fall catalogue on request

cluding wood engravings in black and white and in color; copper engravings; aquatints; bookplates for private collectors and institutions; as well as considerable book illustration and design. Also exhibited was a great variety of his more ephemeral commercial work, such as pamphlets, catalogs, announcements, certificates, and diplomas.

The handsome Grolier Club exhibition catalog, which he designed, contains eight reproductions, some in color and one (printed from the original wood blocks) in three colors, together with an appreciation of the artist by Walter Muir Whitehill, Director of the Boston Athenaeum, and an all too modest note by Ruzicka on his own work. This catalog and *The Wood-Engravings of Rudolph Ruzicka,* a biographical note and critical commentary by W. M. Ivins, Jr., published by the Newark Museum Association in 1917, are recommended for any student of Ruzicka's aims and achievements.

———

In his typographic work, Ruzicka is meticulous and thorough, as befits a master of letter forms. He plans his effects down to the last detail before typesetting begins—all experimenting is done in preliminary layouts and not by resetting galleys of type to develop numerous sample pages.

One of his most interesting assignments a few years ago was to create and develop an entire issue of *The Reader's Digest* to show the possibilities of using considerably more color in that periodical.

To determine exactly what could be done, a specific issue was redesigned and re-created in its entirety. Ruzicka felt that the customary artist's dummy would be insufficient for this demonstration. New and superior layouts were made for every article; each article was reset completely; special art work was commissioned and procured; engravings were made in as many colors as were required; and the entire issue was completely printed and bound with every word of the original text included—not a single word or sentence was cut to achieve an artistic effect.

This special issue was a superb demonstration of what designing brains and taste could do in producing a magazine for mass circulation. The project was of the sort termed "top secret" in the periodical field, and copies of the trial issue are obviously unobtainable . . . even by determined collectors.

While this creative development was going on, production plans to utilize color to this previously undreamed-of degree were also formulated. This production engineering bore fruit recently when the Rumford Press (which prints *The Reader's Digest*) announced the installation of two new five-color Goss presses, each capable of handling a mile of paper in less than four-and-one-half minutes.

Current issues of *The Reader's Digest* reflect a gradually increasing use of color, but as yet they do not approach the design pattern developed by Mr. Ruzicka.

———

Designing THE NEW COLOPHON presented rather different problems, beyond the basic one of intriguing the reading eye by making the "front door" of each article attractive and alluring. The variety of possible solutions is revealed by comparing the first three parts of Volume One with the present issue.

Ruzicka, who doesn't theorize about his work and dislikes talking about it, has followed a course quite unlike his predecessors. His basic idea, obviously, was to decorate and enrich the opening page of each article in a style as far removed as possible from the material used to illustrate it.

As he developed his plan, the seven drawn-decorations hint at the subjects of the

Advertisements

SAWYER'S

If you are not on our mailing list please write for our latest illustrated catalogues.

RARE BOOKS · FINE BINDINGS
SPORTING AND COLOUR PLATE BOOKS

Early English Literature

12-13 GRAFTON ST., NEW BOND ST.

LONDON, W. 1, ENGLAND

CHARLES SCRIBNER'S SONS

597 FIFTH AVENUE　　·.·　　NEW YORK 17, N. Y.

The Rare Book Department carries a large and varied stock of First Editions of English and American Literature, Science, Music, Sport, Literary Manuscripts, Autograph Letters, etc.

DAVID A. RANDALL	JOHN CARTER
NEW YORK	LONDON

articles and are held for the most part in the form of repeat patterns. For the Thoreau article, there is the suggestion of life reflected in Concord River; for the Kipling, an indication of jungle life; for the article of Jefferson and Freneau, the American motif of eagle and column; and so on.

In spite of its diversity, there is integration in the decorative pattern of this Ruzicka-planned issue, from the name line on the title page, with its adjacent abstract decoration, through the front matter, to the oxford-rule pattern for the initial letters and the specially-developed designs for each of the articles. In a sense the decoration is typographic, though only the material used for department headings actually came from the printer's cases. Though the individual elements are conventional, the general style is rather unconventional and to these eyes seems fresh and distinctive.

I can testify to the essential rightness of Ruzicka's solution to a design problem by mentioning details of two books I was privileged to have a hand in some years ago.

The first instance was in connection with a book to greet Bruce Rogers on his return from England in 1935, which was irreverently titled, *Barnacles From Many Bottoms*, with the subtitle "Scraped and Gathered for B.R. by the Typophiles." The book was a cooperative affair, consisting of thirty different signatures, including the contributions of fifty-six individuals. It was done *con amore* and hurriedly, with each individual having complete freedom in carrying out his assignment. The edition comprised 100 copies.

The difficult problem of the title page was welcomed by Mr. Ruzicka—and was his to deal with as he wished. A few days later he thought through to his solution. Could he secure the initials of each of the different contributors to the book, he inquired? The list was furnished, he developed his layout —and an inspired achievement it was.

· EA · VA · JA · EB · PB · PAB · JB · MBC ·
BARNACLES FROM MANY BOTTOMS
SCRAPED AND GATHERED FOR

[decorative initials B R formed from contributor initials]

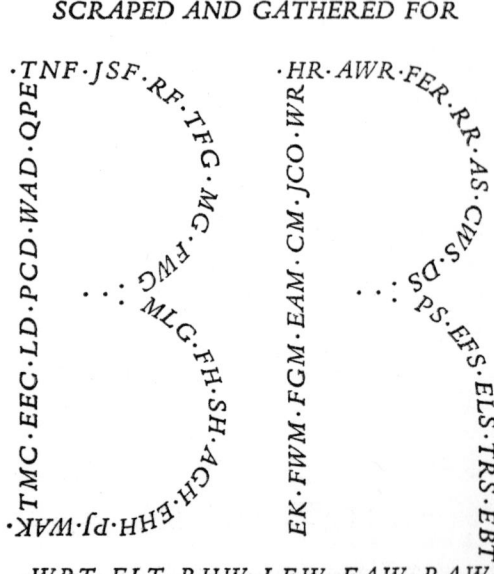

· WRT · ELT · RHW · LFW · EAW · RAW ·
BY THE TYPOPHILES
1935

In working out his plan, he used but one size of Blado italic, forming the heroic initials B R from the initials of thirty-eight of the contributors, and stringing along fourteen more above and below to give the effect of rules. The final four, who came along after the composition was in process, disturbed neither his equanimity nor design one bit— he simply added them on the following page.

The page must be seen in the original to be fully appreciated, for the color pattern, of blue for the initials and black for the re-

ADVERTISEMENTS

Acquire or Dispose of
RARE BOOKS
Manuscripts and other
Literary Property

at the

PARKE-BERNET GALLERIES, Inc.
30 EAST 57 STREET : NEW YORK 22

America's Leading Art and Book Auction House

ARTHUR SWANN, *Vice President*
In Charge of the Book and Print Department

CATALOGUES MAY BE SUBSCRIBED TO BY THE SEASON

LINOTYPE FAIRFIELD

NEITHER publicity nor enthusiastic adjectives are needed to enhance Rudolph Ruzicka's handsome FAIRFIELD type.

Here you see the face in actual use, in typography arranged by Mr. Ruzicka. We need only add that the type is available in seven sizes, 6 to 14 point inclusive, and that a heavier counterpart, Fairfield Medium, is now in process.

LINOTYPE · BROOKLYN 5 · NEW YORK

maining lines and the date, comes off superbly. From conception of idea, to layout, to first proof, everything went according to plan. And Albert Schiller of the Advertising Agencies Service Company solved one of the neatest problems of typesetting in many a week.

The other instance of his happy facility for hitting the target squarely was in connection with the catalog of the Dwiggins exhibition which the American Institute of Graphic Arts sponsored in 1937. This again was a co-operative affair, with signatures arriving from seven different printers. To Ruzicka went the problem of developing the title page—and he supplied a decorative pattern unmistakably Dwiggins in motif, forming the large initials W A D. No other solution could have expressed so succinctly the essence of Dwiggins' decoration.

Elder Colophonians may recall the article in Part Five, "On the Work in Book Illustration of Rudolph Ruzicka" by the late William A. Kittredge, which included two engravings in color (from *New York,* the Grolier Club, 1915, and *Old Houses of Connecticut,* Yale University Press, 1923), together with a reproduction of the decorative half-title of the Limited Editions Club *Fables of La Fontaine,* 1930, an illustration from the Lakeside Press edition of Thoreau's *Walden,* 1930, and two small black and white engravings. It is well worth rereading in addition to the other commentaries previously referred to.

NOTE TO BOOK-BUYERS: Since the previous issue of THE NEW COLOPHON, two books have been published which contain material originally printed in this quarterly. They are David Donald's *Lincoln's Herndon,* with an introduction by Carl Sandburg, published by Knopf; and John Carter's *Taste and Technique in Book Collecting,* published by R. R. Bowker Company. The editors have no hesitation about recommending both volumes.

The publishers, editors, and we hope the subscribers, will carry this joint venture ahead for a second year. Things to look forward to in 1949 are: A superb new cover design by T. M. Cleland, which ranks with his very best decorative work . . . An article on the Grabhorns, their methods, their friends, and their productions, by Oscar Lewis . . . The intriguing results of THE NEW COLOPHON's Immortality Poll . . . An account of the making of paste papers, with a handsome example especially made for us by the author, Rosamond B. Loring . . . Stephen Vincent Benét's own story of the genesis and development of *John Brown's Body* . . . The overall design for Part Five, which will be developed by the eminent calligrapher, Oscar Ogg . . . A survey of the literature of the Gold Rush by Carl I. Wheat . . . The true story of Benjamin Franklin's famous "printer" epitaph, by Lyman Butterfield . . . Vincent Starrett's offering of some by-products of book-madness . . . And many more.

PAUL A. BENNETT

ADVERTISEMENTS

> "In this connection, we would be remiss not to acknowledge in print our colossal debt to HOUSE OF EL DIEFF (Lew D. Feldman), 45 East 51 Street, New York 22, New York, the foremost dealer in the world specializing in detective first editions and manuscripts. Without the help of HOUSE OF EL DIEFF these choice copies could never have been gathered under one ratiocinative roof."
>
> ELLERY QUEEN

Our collection consists of approximately three thousand First Editions, and several choice Manuscripts: — The MS. of *A Scandal of Bohemia*, the FIRST Sherlock Holmes short story; the MS. of Mark Twain's *A Double Barrelled Detective Story*, now available for purchase for the first time since 1910; the complete MS. of *The Valley of Fear*, the ONLY Sherlock Holmes novel that can be acquired today, etc., etc.

and now:

We have an ambitious plan for a *Catalogue* to be issued on the 100th anniversary of the death of Edgar A. Poe, October, 1949. Anyone interested in making long range reservations, please write, no obligation of course.

HOUSE OF EL DIEFF
45 EAST 51 · NEW YORK 22, N. Y.

Addenda to the List of
BOOKS ABOUT BOOKS, 1947

The list of "Books about Books, 1947" (printed in the previous issue of THE NEW COLOPHON) brought forth several helpful letters which contained information concerning further "books about books" published both in 1947 and 1948. One writer urged strongly that the prices of the various books be included in the entries; this seems a good idea, and it will probably be adopted for the 1948 list.

Two additional titles for 1947 follow:

BINING, ARTHUR C., and others. *Writings on Pennsylvania History, a Bibliography. A List of Secondary Materials Compiled under the Auspices of the Pennsylvania Historical Association By Arthur C. Bining ... Robert L. Brunhouse ... Norman B. Wilkinson....* Pennsylvania Historical and Museum Commission, Harrisburg, 1946 [published in 1947]. xxxviii, [2], 565 pp.

Comprises 6,165 brief entries of separately-printed items and periodical articles, arranged under subjects. There is an author index at the end.

DAHL, FOLKE. *Dutch Corantos 1618-1650. A Bibliography illustrated with 334 Facsimile Reproductions of Corantos Printed 1618-1625. And an Introductory Essay on 17th Century Stop Press News.* Printed (at Gothenburg) for The Koninklijke Bibliotheek, The Hague. 87, [7] pp.

A basic bibliographical tool for the study of the earliest Dutch newspapers. More than 2,300 different numbers are enumerated and located. There are short biographies of all publishers and printers of these corantos. There are also short introductory essays sketching the evolution of 16 different papers. The facsimile reproductions are nine-tenths the size of the originals.

Unfortunately I have not yet had the opportunity of examining a copy of Mr. Dahl's work. The entry and annotation have been accepted on faith from the author.

GEORGE L. McKAY

Advertisements

JAMES F. DRAKE
INCORPORATED

First Editions · Rare Books
Autographs · Manuscripts

24 West 40th Street
NEW YORK 18, N. Y.

Edition exhausted?

Whenever a first printing is exhausted it is possible to make a reprinting by offset lithography. For a number of years, publishers have welcomed the economy of our service in meeting special needs.

DUENEWALD
Printing Corporation

738 GREENWICH STREET
NEW YORK 14, N. Y.

DISTRIBUTORS

Andria, Arak, Archer, Brooke, W&A All Rag, Westerly, and standard Mill Brand papers.

• • •

WHITEHEAD & ALLIGER Co.
INC.

ELEVEN THOMAS STREET
NEW YORK 7, N. Y.

A GUIDE TO MAKING BOOKS

Are you preparing a manuscript for the press? Here printing processes, printer's terms, and proofreader's marks are concisely explained. Are you choosing a format? Here are many kinds of specimen pages and a discussion of book design. Here are information and inspiration for the editor, designer, and publisher.

Written and designed by
PAUL McPHARLIN

For your post-free copy send $2.50 to
The NORTH RIVER PRESS
311-319 West 43rd St., New York 18, N. Y.

Notes About Contributors

CURT F. BÜHLER is Keeper of Printed Books at the Pierpont Morgan Library, New York, and a frequent contributor to bibliographical publications.

DeLANCEY FERGUSON has been chairman of the English Department at Brooklyn College since 1944. He is the author of interpretative biographies of Robert Burns and Mark Twain, and was an occasional contributor to the original *Colophon*.

BARROWS MUSSEY described his original collection of books on the publishing trade in "The Renegade Bibliophobe," in Vol. III, No. 2 of *The Colophon,* New Series, 1938. He has been printer, publisher, magazine editor, literary agent, author of several illustrated books about New England, translator into English from seven languages, writer on conjuring, and *ghost*-writer of a book on spiritualism.

WILLIAM PEDEN is associate professor of English at the University of Missouri, and director of the Missouri Writers' Workshop. His doctor's dissertation at the University of Virginia was entitled *Thomas Jefferson: Book Collector*. He is the author of *Some Aspects of Jefferson Bibliography,* and co-author of *The Life and Selected Writings of Thomas Jefferson* and *Selected Writings of John and John Quincy Adams*.

J. E. SCOTT, in the course of twenty-five years, has assembled a Rider Haggard collection second to none. His authoritative Haggard bibliography was published in England this year, and he is now bringing to completion a bibliography of Stanley J. Weyman.

BOYD B. STUTLER has been managing editor of the *American Legion Magazine* since 1936, and served as a war correspondent in the Pacific-Asiatic theater. He says that he has been "fussing with the John Brown theme" for nearly forty years.

JAMES E. THORPE, JR., returned in 1946 to the Department of English at Princeton University from a five-year tour of duty with the Army Air Forces, during which he rose to the rank of colonel. He was recently named assistant dean of the Graduate School at Princeton.

JAMES PLAYSTED WOOD, editor of the annual volumes in the Funk & Wagnalls Centenary Series in American Literature, is the author of *American Magazines: Their Social and Economic Influence,* which will be published early in 1949. His "English and American Criticism of Thoreau" was published in *The New England Quarterly* in 1933.

ADVERTISEMENTS

QUARITCH
Established 1847

AMERICANA
BIBLIOGRAPHY, BOTANICAL WORKS
EARLY SCIENTIFIC WORKS
ENGLISH LITERATURE OF THE
15TH TO 20TH CENTURY
EUROPEAN HISTORY, FINE ARTS
FINE BINDINGS
ILLUMINATED MANUSCRIPTS
INCUNABULA, NATURAL HISTORY
SPORTING BOOKS, ETC.

Classified Catalogues sent post free on request.

BERNARD QUARITCH Ltd.
11 GRAFTON ST., NEW BOND ST.,
LONDON, W. 1, ENGLAND

THE
ANTHOENSEN PRESS
PORTLAND, MAINE

Offers unusual facilities in equipment and in personnel for the production of

BOOKS, PAMPHLETS, AND
PERIODICAL PUBLICATIONS

Also many kinds of miscellaneous literary, institutional, and commercial printing are undertaken. In the printing of Bibliographies the Press provides a degree of efficiency and accuracy not often obtained in this class of work. All work is carefully designed and supervised. Enquiries receive prompt attention.

You who read this are probably a *Charter Subscriber* of THE NEW COLOPHON. Your friends may still become Charter Subscribers. A few sets of Volume I, Parts 1, 2, 3, and 4, are still available at $15.00.

Order from your bookseller.

PHILIP C. DUSCHNES

FIRST EDITIONS
FINE PRESS BOOKS

Catalogues issued frequently

66 EAST 56TH STREET
NEW YORK 22, N. Y.

INDEX · THE NEW COLOPHON · VOLUME I

Part 1, pp. 1-108 Part 2, pp. 109-216 Part 3, pp. 217-316 Part 4, pp. 317-427

....

ADDENDUM TO "ENEMIES OF BOOKS," AN. Michael Sadleir   235
Adler, Elmer. NOTE TO COMMEMORATE THE 150TH ANNIVERSARY OF LITHOGRAPHY   366
Advertisers, List of   427
"Ah Sin—A Drama" Bret Harte and Samuel L. Clemens   132, 133
Almanacs, Early American   296-298
ALMOST BOOKS. Frederick R. Goff   125
AMERICAN ACADEMY OF ARTS AND LETTERS, AWARD OF GOLD MEDAL TO BRUCE ROGERS   306, 308, 310
Anthoensen, Fred. Designer Parts 1 and 3; Printer of 1, 2, 3, and 4; Note about   100, 102
Appeals, listed   426
Appleton, Leroy H. Cover design, Parts 1, 2, 3, and 4; Note about   102
Bailey, Lydia   394-400
Bennett, Paul A. MARGINALIA   100, 208, 306, 408
Bentley, Richard   245-255
Bibliographies published during 1947   281, 282, 283
BIBLIOPHILE, THE PINCHPENNY. Barrows Mussey   383
Biemiller, Reynard. Nameplate   102
Birss, John H. "A MERE SALE TO EFFECT"   239
Blanck, Jacob. WHERE THERE'S A WILL....   47
Boas, George. SILHOUETTE OF A LIBRARIAN   151
Book illustration, books about, published in 1947   289

BOOK IS A BOOK IS A BOOK, A. Donald C. Gallup   67
BOOKS ABOUT BOOKS, 1947   280
    ADDENDA TO   420
    Compiled by George L. McKay
Books of varying degrees of rarity   135-150
Books on miscellaneous subjects pertaining to making of books, published during 1947   290
Books read and owned by Puritans   13-26
"Boy's Will, A," by Robert Frost   6
Brodhead, John R.   240-245
BROWN, JOHN: HIS HAND AND PEN. Boyd B. Stutler   321
Brown, John, his letters, autographs, and friends   321-334
Bühler, Curt F. ROBERT WALDEGRAVE AND THE PIRATES OF DUNKIRK   377
Calligraphy and Lettering, books about, published during 1947   287
Capon, Charles R. Headpiece   100
Carter, John. REFLECTIONS ON RARITY   134
Catalogues of Exhibitions, published during 1947   284, 285
Cleland, T. M. Design Part 2; Note about   208-214
Clemens, Samuel L. "Ah Sin—A Drama" with Bret Harte   132, 133
    "Tom Sawyer" (as a play)   132
Collectors and collecting, books about, published during 1947   286, 287
Colophon, The. Data concerning publication   104
COURT OF APPEALS, THE. David A. Randall   81, 190, 291, 401
    Appeals listed   426

423

Index

Cover Design, Parts 1, 2, 3, and 4. Leroy H. Appleton
Crane, Stephen   33, 115-123, 402
CRANE, STEPHEN, WAR CORRESPONDENT. Ames W. Williams   113
Cuno, Theodore   366
"Dance of Death" by Hans Holbein   161
Denby, Ellen. GRANDFATHER WAS A COLLECTOR   271
Donald, David. THE TRUE STORY OF "HERNDON'S LINCOLN"   221
DRIFTING INTO A PRINT COLLECTION. Allen Evarts Foster   36
Dwiggins, W. A. Colophon device   100
EARLY FROST BROADSIDE, AN. Lawrance Thompson   5
Evans, Lieutenant H. E., Letter to Elbert Hubbard   34
Ferguson, DeLancey. "THE PEN TOOK CHARGE"   335
FINDINGS OF THE COURT   84, 195, 293, 402
Fish, Williston. The Last Will and Testament of Charles Lounsbury   48
Foster, Allen Evarts. DRIFTING INTO A PRINT COLLECTION   36
FRENEAU, JEFFERSON, AND THE *Poems* OF 1809. William Peden   394
Frost, Robert   5-12
    "A Boy's Will"   6
    Longfellow-Frost Association   6
    "The Later Minstrel"   7-12
Gallup, Donald C. A BOOK IS A BOOK IS A BOOK   67
GHOST FROM A BARBER SHOP, A. Carl J. Weber   185
Goff, Frederick R. ALMOST BOOKS   125
Goudy, Frederic W.   100
Government Printing Office   264-270
G. P. O. IN WAR AND PEACE, THE. Cedric Larson   264
GRANDFATHER WAS A COLLECTOR. Ellen Denby   271

Haggard, H. Rider   348-356
Hamilton, Sinclair. HOMER MARTIN AS ILLUSTRATOR   256
Hardy, Thomas   84, 85, 185-189
HARMLESS DRUDGE, THIS. Herman W. Liebert   175
Hart, James D. A PURITAN BOOKSHELF   13
Harte, Bret. "Ah Sin—A Drama" with Samuel L. Clemens   132, 133, 401-403
HATCHERS-OUT OF TALES. J. E. Scott   348
Heraldic device   304
Herndon, William   221-234
Hershfield, Leo. Illustrations for GRANDFATHER WAS A COLLECTOR   271
"Historiarum Veteris Instrumenti Icones"   161-174
Hofer, Philip. HOLBEIN'S OLD TESTAMENT WOODCUTS   161
HOLBEIN'S OLD TESTAMENT WOODCUTS. Philip Hofer   161
HOMER MARTIN AS ILLUSTRATOR. Sinclair Hamilton   256
Hubbard, Elbert   27-35
HUBBARD, ELBERT, AND "A MESSAGE TO GARCIA." Dard Hunter   27
Hunter, Dard. ELBERT HUBBARD AND "A MESSAGE TO GARCIA"   27
IMMORTALITY POLL   314
Imprinted papers, cards, currency, mottoes, prize cards, shinplasters   300, 302
"In the Sierras; or The Luck of Roaring Camp" A Play. Bret Harte   132
JEFFERSON, FRENEAU, AND THE *Poems* OF 1809. William Peden   394
JOHN BROWN: HIS HAND AND PEN. Boyd B. Stutler   321
Johnson, John, collector of fugitive printing   86
Kent, Rockwell. Vignette on title-pages, Parts 1, 2, 3, 4
Kipling, Rudyard
    Friendship with Rider Haggard   348-356
    Poems and stories influencing him   335-348

INDEX

KIPLING, RUDYARD: TWO FOOTNOTES
   1. "The Pen Took Charge." DeLancey Ferguson   335
   2. Hatchers-out of Tales. J. E. Scott   348
Labels, binders', booksellers', and printers'   86, 200, 304
Landauer, Bella C., collection of American advertising printing   86-94
Larson, Cedric. THE G. P. O. IN WAR AND PEACE   264
"Later Minstrel, The"   7-12
Letterheads, collecting of   199, 200
Liebert, Herman W. THIS HARMLESS DRUDGE   175
Lincoln, Abraham   221-234
LITHOGRAPH. Benton Spruance   facing 366
LITHOGRAPHY, NOTE TO COMMEMORATE ANNIVERSARY. Elmer Adler   366
Longfellow, Henry Wadsworth   6, 7
Lounsbury, Charles, last will and testament   47, 48, 51, 53-57
McKay, George L. ADDENDA TO THE LIST OF BOOKS ABOUT BOOKS   420
   BOOKS ABOUT BOOKS, 1947   280
McPharlin, Paul. A SCRAPBOOK OF STRAYS   86, 198, 296
   Paul McPharlin—1903-1948   408
Manuscripts, books about, published during 1947   287
MARGINALIA. Paul A. Bennett   100, 208, 306, 408
MARTIN, HOMER, AS ILLUSTRATOR. Sinclair Hamilton   256
Melville, Herman   239-255
"MERE SALE TO EFFECT, A." Edited by John H. Birss   239
"'Message to Garcia, A': A Bibliographical Puzzle"   31
Milton, John, inscriptions and autographs   357-365

MR. THOREAU WRITES A BOOK. James Playsted Wood   367
Mug Books   202, 204, 206
Mussey, Barrows. THE PINCHPENNY BIBLIOPHILE   383
Newspapers and Periodicals, books about, published during 1947   285, 286
NOTES ABOUT CONTRIBUTORS   104, 214, 310, 418
"Omoo" Herman Melville   239-255
Paper, books about, published during 1947   289, 290
Paradise Lost   357
Peden, William. JEFFERSON, FRENEAU, AND THE *Poems* OF 1809   394
"PEN TOOK CHARGE, THE." DeLancey Ferguson   335
PINCHPENNY BIBLIOPHILE, THE. Barrows Mussey   383
PIRATES OF DUNKIRK, THE, AND ROBERT WALDEGRAVE. Curt F. Bühler   377
Pollard, Alfred W.   151-159
"PRESENTATION" *Paradise Lost,* THE. James Thorpe   357
Prince, Oliver Hillhouse   185-189
Printers and Printing, books about, published during 1947   287-289
Publishing and bookselling, books about, published during 1947   289
PURITAN BOOKSHELF, A. James D. Hart   13
Pytlak, Leonard. Original Serigraph   facing 62
Randall, David A. THE COURT OF APPEALS & FINDINGS OF THE COURT   81, 190, 291, 401
REFLECTIONS ON RARITY. John Carter   134
ROBERT WALDEGRAVE AND THE PIRATES OF DUNKIRK. Curt F. Bühler   377
Rogers, Bruce   306, 308, 310, 414
Rowan, Captain A. S.   32, 33
Roycroft Shop, productions of   28, 29, 32, 34

RUDYARD KIPLING: TWO FOOTNOTES
 1. "The Pen Took Charge." DeLancey Ferguson ... 335
 2. Hatchers-out of Tales. J. E. Scott ... 348
Ruzicka, Rudolph. Design Part 4; Note on ... 410
Sadleir, Michael. ADDENDUM TO "ENEMIES OF BOOKS" ... 235
Scott, J. E. HATCHERS-OUT OF TALES ... 348
SCRAPBOOK OF STRAYS, A. Paul McPharlin ... 86, 198, 296
Senefelder, Alois ... 366
Serigraph, An Original. Leonard Pytlak ... *facing* 62
SILHOUETTE OF A LIBRARIAN. George Boas ... 151
Smedley, Menella ... 337, 346, 348
Special Collections, Books about, published during 1947 ... 283, 284
Spruance, Benton. Lithograph Proof, signed ... *facing* 366
Stamps, postage ... 94, 96
STEPHEN CRANE, WAR CORRESPONDENT. Ames W. Williams ... 113
Stutler, Boyd B. JOHN BROWN: HIS HAND AND PEN ... 321
TEN YEARS OF SERIGRAPHY. Carl Zigrosser ... 58
Theatre sheets ... 96, 98
THIS HARMLESS DRUDGE. Herman W. Liebert ... 175
Thompson, Lawrance. AN EARLY FROST BROADSIDE ... 5
Thoreau, Henry ... 367-376
Thorpe, James. THE "PRESENTATION" *Paradise Lost* ... 357
Tinker, Chauncey P. Citation of American Academy of Arts and Letters Gold Medal Award to Bruce Rogers ... 306, 308
Title-pages for copyright purpose ... 125-133
"*Tom Sawyer. A Play in 4 Acts.*" Samuel L. Clemens ... 132

TRUE STORY OF "HERNDON'S LINCOLN," THE. David Donald ... 221
"*Trumpet-Major, The,*" Thomas Hardy ... 186, 187
Vail, Dr. R. W. G. ... 31
WALDEGRAVE, ROBERT, AND THE PIRATES OF DUNKIRK. Curt F. Bühler ... 377
Weber, Carl J. A GHOST FROM A BARBER SHOP ... 185
Webster, Noah, prime mover in establishment and adoption of copyright laws ... 125
"*Week on the Concord and Merrimack Rivers, A.*" ... 367-376
Weik, Jesse William ... 221-234
WHERE THERE'S A WILL .... Jacob Blanck ... 47
Williams, Ames W. STEPHEN CRANE, WAR CORRESPONDENT ... 113
Wilson, Carroll A. ... 102
Wood, James Playsted. MR. THOREAU WRITES A BOOK ... 367
Zigrosser, Carl. TEN YEARS OF SERIGRAPHY ... 58

APPEALS AND FINDINGS OF THE COURT OF APPEALS

Adams, John Quincy. Letters to his son on Bible study ... 195, 197
"Aeneas Africanus" ... 82, 84, 85
Bret Harte in Sunlight ... 401, 403
Brontë's, Anne, "The Tenant of Wildfell Hall" ... 194, 196
Burns, Robert, and The Scots Musical Museum ... 190, 193
Cinderella ... 83, 85
Crane, Stephen, "Whilomville Stories" ... 293, 402
Doyle, A. Conan, "A Study in Scarlet" ... 401, 403
"Enchanted Shirt, The," John Hay's ... 194, 196
English Drama, 1660-1700 ... 84

INDEX

Frank Forester, Engraver? 291, 292, 295
"Great Expectations," Rarity of 402
Hay's, John, "The Enchanted Shirt" 194, 196
Henty, G. A. 83, 84, 85
Irving, Washington, "Salmagundi"
　291, 293, 295
Letters to his son on Bible study. John
　Quincy Adams 195, 197
Percy's "Reliques" and its cancel leaves 404
Praepinguida, The 83
"Reliques of Ancient English Poetry"
　and its cancel leaves 404
"Renaissance in Italy," J. A. Symonds 193, 194
"Rock me to Sleep" 401, 403
Roentgen's Announcement of the X-Ray
　195, 197
"Salmagundi," Washington Irving's
　291, 293, 295
School Press Products 292
Showing off, or Helpful? 292, 295
Smith, Adam, "Wealth of Nations"
　193, 195, 196
Steinbeck Firsts, Variant bindings on 401, 404
"Study in Scarlet, A," Doyle's 401, 403
Symonds, John Addington, "Renaissance in Italy" 193, 194
"Tenant of Wildfell Hall, The," Anne
　Brontë 194, 196
"Three Bears, The" 292
"Wealth of Nations," Adam Smith
　193, 195, 196
X-Ray Announcement, Roentgen 195, 197

ADVERTISERS

Abraham Lincoln Book Shop 103
Anthoensen Press, The 201, 303, 421
Associated American Artists 311
Berès, Pierre, Inc. 213
Bittner, H., and Co. 205
Bowker, R. R., Company 91, 203
Curtis Paper Company 107
Denny, E. & K. 93
Doubleday & Co., Inc. 409
Drake, James F., Inc. 93, 213, 299, 419
Duenewald Printing Corporation
　107, 201, 303, 419
Duschnes, Crawford Inc. 215, 421
Duschnes, Philip C. 103, 309, 421
Golden Eagle Press, The 101
House of El Dieff 95, 211, 301, 417
Knopf, Alfred A. 97, 207, 305, 411
Krucraft Leather Co. 303
Linotype 107, 201, 313, 415
North River Press, The 307, 419
Oxford University Press 409
Parke-Bernet Galleries, Inc. 89, 209, 299, 415
Princeton University Press 105
Quaritch, Bernard, Ltd. 209, 307, 421
Riley, Frank H. 213
Rinehart & Company 299
Robinson, William H., Ltd. 205
Rogers, Arthur 99
Sawyer's 99, 307, 413
Scribner's, Charles, Sons 103, 209, 313, 413
Serigraph Galleries 99
Stevens-Nelson Paper Corporation, The
　213, 303
Story Classics 409
Taylor & Taylor, Printers 93
University of Pittsburgh Press, The 205
Whitehead & Alliger Co., Inc. 419
Wreden, William P. 93
Yellow Hall, The 99